Debra K. Farrington is the author of seven books on Christian spirituality including *Hearing with the Heart* and *Unceasing Prayer*. A popular retreat leader and speaker, Debra also writes for a variety of magazines and is a member of the Episcopal Network for Animal Welfare. She lives in Pennsylvania with her family, which includes six cats and a dog. For more information about Debra's speaking events or to contact her, please visit www.debrafarrington.com.

A percentage of the author's profits on this book
will be donated to PAWS of Central Pennsylvania,
a no-kill animal rescue and spay/neuter group.

ALL GOD'S CREATURES

The Blessing of Animal Companions

DEBRA K. FARRINGTON

PARACLETE PRESS
Brewster, Massachusetts

ALL GOD'S CREATURES: The Blessing of Animal Companions

2006 First Printing
Copyright © 2006 by Debra K. Farrington
ISBN 1-55725-472-9

  Library of Congress Cataloging-in-Publication Data
Farrington, Debra K.
  All God's creatures : the blessing of animal companions / Debra
K. Farrington.
     p. cm.
  ISBN 1-55725-472-9
  1. Animals--Religious aspects--Christianity. 2. Pets--Religious
aspects--Christianity. I. Title.
  BT746.F37 2006
  241'.693--dc22
                                    2006014534
10 9 8 7 6 5 4 3 2 1

Published by Paraclete Press
Brewster, Massachusetts
www.paracletepress.com

Printed in the United States of America

To Marley, and to all the animals

"Far too often, Christians have accepted the common secular view that we are the masters of animals, their rulers or owners—utterly forgetting that the dominion promised to humanity is a deputized dominion, in which we are to stand before creation as God's vice-regents, putting into effect not our own egotistical wants but God's own law of love and mercy. . . . For if animals are God's creatures, we have no absolute rights over them, only the duty to look after them as God would look after them."[1]

—Andrew Linzey

"[I]n the vivid contemplation and knowledge of the creatures, the soul sees with great clearness that there is in them such abundance of graces and virtues and beauty wherewith God endowed them, that, as it seems to her, they are all clothed with marvelous natural beauty, derived from and communicated by that infinite supernatural beauty of the image of God, whose beholding of them clothes the world and all the heavens with beauty and joy...."[2]

—St. John of the Cross

ᴓᴓᴓᴓ

"*Ethics are responsibility without limits towards all that lives. As a general proposition, the definition of ethics as relationship within a disposition to reverence for life does not make a very moving impression. But it is the only complete one. Compassion is too narrow to take as the total essence of the ethical. It denotes, of course, only interest in the suffering will-to-live. But ethics include also feeling as one's own all the circumstances and all the aspirations of the will-to-live, its pleasure too, and its longing to live itself out to the full, as well as its urge to self-perfecting.*"[3]

—Albert Schweitzer

"[O]ur work for animals ties in with the very purpose of our lives and our eternal destiny. It means for us humane work is not an isolated merciful activity, an occupation to fill spare time, but something which invites the co-operation of all our powers of soul and body. Because, since God made all the animals and they are His, the more we imitate the attributes of God in our approach to them and see things as He does the better we are able to serve His creatures of which He has put us in charge. The holier we are, then the more our sympathy with animals increases, as the Saints showed, the better Christians we prove ourselves to be."[4]

—Dom Ambrose Agius, OSB

CONTENTS

PART ONE

In the Beginning . . .

But ask the animals, and they will teach you;

the birds of the air, and they will tell you;

ask the plants of the earth, and they will teach you;

and the fish of the sea will declare to you.

Who among all these does not know that the hand of the

Lord has done this?

In his hand is the life of every living thing and the breath

of every human being.

—Job 12:7–10

few years ago one of my cats jumped up on my lap while I was saying morning prayers. After I pushed him away I realized I'd done something quite wrong. "Come, Lord Jesus," were my words, while my actions said: "but don't sit on my lap!"

Now, before you start worrying about me, I know that my cat isn't Jesus. But I do believe that if God created everything—if God breathed life into all of creation—that I'm just as likely to encounter God's presence in a cat, dog, or some other animal as I am in a human being. Centuries ago a frog taught St. Benno the same lesson. This wise bishop was walking in the fields praying, as was his custom, but a noisy frog kept interrupting him. Finally Benno ordered the frog to be quiet, and the frog ceased his croaking. (I'm continually amazed that animals obeyed the people in these ancient stories without question, but that's a question for another day.) As he walked in the silence, however, Benno began to wonder if God might not find the frog's song just as, or more, agreeable than Benno's own, and so he commanded the frog to sing again. The air was filled with the prayers of the priest and the frog, and God was pleased.

This ancient tale recognizing the place and importance of the animals isn't an anomaly. There are many stories from our Christian ancestors—including the Desert Fathers and Mothers, and the Celts—that display great affection and respect for the animal kingdom; you'll find many of them in these pages. But St. Benno's struggle to let the animals be all that God intended them to be, instead of viewing them as lesser creatures, is still ours today. While writing this book I have discovered that some church folks as well as some who care for animals view my work with a bit of suspicion. Some veterinarians and animal trainers wonder why I would want to bring religion into the conversation, while those who love the church wonder why I think animals should find a place in our life and prayers. More than once, in the writing of this book, people have asked me how I understand the Bible's statement that *people* are made in the image of God, while it doesn't say the same for animals (Genesis 1:27). There are several answers to that question. First, we are animals, just like those creatures we like to separate ourselves from. Remembering that ought to bring just a little bit of humility to bear on the question. "[W]hatever else we want to say about the meaning of being made in the image of God," church historian Roberta Bondi writes, "our tradition is also very clear that it isn't only human beings who reflect who God is. All of creation, every bit of it, expresses God and points us back to God."[5]

The second answer is that, if we're made in the image of God then we ought to love what God loves, which is all of creation. Or in the words of the fourth-century St. Gregory of Nyssa: "For when he considers the universe can anyone be so simple-minded as not to believe that the Divine is present in everything, pervading, embracing and penetrating it? For all things depend upon Him who is, and nothing can exist which does not have its being in Him who is."[6]

The book of Genesis tells the story of God's creating the world, day by day. On the fifth and sixth days God created the birds, the fish, and the animals who walk the earth, and all of them are good in God's eyes. God even instructs every created being, including humans, to eat only plants (Genesis 1:30) rather than each other, though this instruction changed after the Flood. But God creates and delights in all that exists, and gives "dominion" of the earth to human beings. The word "dominion" has frequently been used as justification to do whatever we wish with the animals; for some the word *dominion* implies that animals exist only for the use of people. But biblical scholars tell us that this is a misinterpretation of that word. When God gives people dominion over the animals, God is asking us to care for the animals in the same way God cares for us. We are to be God's shepherds for the animals—creatures God made, just as God made us—making sure that they are safe and provided for in the same way a shepherd cares for his sheep.

Later in the Bible, God becomes angry with the people and floods the world. But before doing that God saves Noah and his family and two of each kind of animal. If God created all that exists, made an effort to save all of it, and continues to love all of it, who are we to abuse it? If we are made in the image of God, we are asked to behave like God toward and with all of creation.

This isn't some oddball or new fangled idea. As far back as the earliest Christian centuries Christians began praying for the animals. St. Basil, one of the early church fathers, thought of the animals as his brothers. "O God, enlarge within us the sense of fellowship with all living things," he prayed, "our brothers the animals to whom thou gavest the earth as their home in common with us." Fourth-century St. Gregory Nazianzen, too, prayed for the animals as fellow creatures of God:

> You alone are unutterable, from the times you created all things that can be spoken of.
> You alone are unknowable, from the time you created all things that can be known.
> All things cry out about you; those which speak, and those which cannot speak.
> All things honor you; those which think, and those which cannot think.

For there is one longing, one groaning, that all things have for
you. . . .

All things pray to you that comprehend your plan, and offer
you a silent hymn.

In you, the One, all things abide, and all things endlessly run to
you who are the end of all.[7]

—St. Gregory Nazianzen

These early Christians sensed that the animals were, in St. Basil's
words, brothers and sisters. They are creatures given existence by
the same Creator who breathed life into us. In one imaginative
re-telling of the Genesis story for children, Jewish author Nancy
Sohn Swartz even imagines God consulting the animals about making
humans, and the animals suggesting all sorts of qualities that
humans ought to have.[8] The tiger wants God to make people brave,
the lamb wants them to be gentle, and so on.

The same understanding is found in ancient Christian writings,
like that of thirteenth-century St. Bonaventure, who wrote:

The creatures of the sense world signify the invisible attributes
of God, partly because God is the origin, exemplar and end of
every creature, and every effect is the sign of its cause, the
exemplification of its exemplar and the path to the end, to
which it leads. . . . For every creature is by its nature a kind of
effigy and likeness of the eternal Wisdom.

Therefore, open your eyes, alert the ears of your spirit, open your lips and apply your heart so that in all creatures you may see, hear, praise, love and worship, glorify and honor your God.[9]

Centuries later, the Russian novelist Fyodor Dostoevsky would echo a very similar sentiment in *The Brothers Karamozov*, when Father Zossima speaks these words:

Brothers, be not afraid of men's sins. Love man even in his sin, for that already bears the semblance of divine love and is the highest love on earth. Love all God's creatures, the whole of it and every grain of sand. Love every leaf, every ray of God's light! Love the animals, love the plants, love everything. And if you love everything you will perceive the divine mystery in things. And once you have perceived it, you will begin to comprehend it ceaselessly more and more every day. And you will at last come to love the whole world with an abiding, universal love.[10]

My own study leads me to believe that God created—in some way, shape, or form—all that exists, and that God didn't just stop loving all of it once it came into being. I don't know if God plays favorites and likes people better than animals, though I suspect not. If people were, indeed, made in the image of God, and given the responsibility to care for the earth that God dreams of (Genesis 1:26), then we have responsibilities for the animals—all of them—beginning with the ones we bring into our homes.

Animals and Humans in the Hebrew Scriptures

Perhaps some of our own ambivalence about calling the animals our kin comes from the Bible, which, it must be admitted, gives mixed messages about the value of animals. On one hand, as already mentioned, Scripture points to God's love for the animals. As they are created, God declares them all good:

> And God said, "Let the waters bring forth swarms of living creatures, and let birds fly above the earth across the dome of the sky." So God created the great sea monsters and every living creature that moves, of every kind, with which the waters swarm, and every winged bird of every kind. And God saw that it was good. God blessed them, saying, "Be fruitful and multiply and fill the waters in the seas, and let birds multiply on the earth." And there was evening and there was morning, the fifth day.
>
> And God said, "Let the earth bring forth living creatures of every kind: cattle and creeping things and wild animals of the earth of every kind." And it was so. God made the wild animals of the earth of every kind, and the cattle of every kind, and

everything that creeps upon the ground of every kind. And God saw that it was good.

—Genesis 1:20–25

Later, God is said to literally flood the earth, saving only a representative portion of the creatures that were created. Following this scene of what must have been horrible, worldwide tsunami-like devastation, God covenants not only with Noah and the human race, but with all the animals as well.

Then God said to Noah and to his sons with him, "As for me, I am establishing my covenant with you and your descendants after you, *and with every living creature that is with you, the birds, the domestic animals, and every animal of the earth with you*, as many as came out of the ark. I establish my covenant with you, that never again shall all flesh be cut off by the waters of a flood, and never again shall there be a flood to destroy the earth."

—Genesis 9:8–11 [italics mine]

Within the Psalms we find various pastoral references to the animals. Psalm 36 echoes God's love for the animals, as well as the humans, following the Flood: "Your righteousness is like the mighty mountains, your judgments are like the great deep; you save humans and animals alike, O LORD" (Psalm 36:6). Loving images of the animals are found in other psalms as well, most notably in Psalm 104, which paints the picture of humans and animals being cared for by a loving God. Psalms 147 and 148 give us a sense of God's love and care for the animals as well.

Perhaps one of the best known and most poetic images related to animals in the Bible is that of the peaceable kingdom:

> The wolf shall live with the lamb, the leopard shall lie down with the kid, the calf and the lion and the fatling together, and a little child shall lead them. The cow and the bear shall graze, their young shall lie down together; and the lion shall eat straw like the ox. The nursing child shall play over the hole of the asp, and the weaned child shall put its hand on the adder's den.
>
> —Isaiah 11:6–8

In this passage the prophet Isaiah speaks of a time yet to come, when peace will be restored on earth, where not only will people live together in harmony, but even the animals will stop eating one another and lie down together.

These lovely, often bucolic images are balanced, however, with stories of animal sacrifice and destruction. At the same time that God covenants with Noah and the animals, God tells Noah that "[t]he fear and dread of you shall rest on every animal of the earth, and on every bird of the air, on everything that creeps on the ground, and on all the fish of the sea" (Genesis 9:2). God explicitly gives Noah and his descendents permission to eat the animals, albeit with certain provisions still observed in Jewish law today. Animal sacrifice is assumed in the Hebrew Scriptures. When God intervenes as Abraham starts to sacrifice his son Isaac, God provides a ram as sacrifice instead. The message is unambiguous: Animals are expendable, while human children are not. So, while God covenants with the animals, and asks people to care for them as God would, there are also scenes of sacrifice and terror that balance the more pastoral scenes.

Humans and Animals in the Christian Testament

We don't have many passages that tell us about Jesus' relationship with animals in the Christian Scriptures, but there are at least a few tantalizing tidbits. Although it is not recorded in Scripture, we commonly picture Jesus at his birth in the manger surrounded by animals. "From the second century onwards," theologian Alister McGrath writes, "commentators on the birth of Christ linked the scene with Isaiah 1:3, which speaks of the ox and the ass knowing their true master and his crib. It seems that this prophetic passage was then linked with the birth of Christ, thus reminding us that the whole of the created order is involved in the birth of Christ and the new creation which will result from his incarnation, death, and resurrection."[11]

Mark reports that Jesus was attended by the wild beasts as he fasted in the desert for forty days following his baptism (Mark 1:13). Jesus himself seems to use the imagery of a hen in an affectionate way in Matthew 23:37: "Jerusalem, Jerusalem, the city that kills the prophets and stones those who are sent to it! How often have I desired to gather your children together as a hen gathers her brood under her wings, and you were not willing!" Jesus, of course, is understood to be the Lion of Judah, and the Lamb of God. In John, we find Jesus comparing himself to the serpent that Moses lifted up for the Israelites in the wilderness in order that the people might live: "And just as Moses lifted up the serpent in the wilderness, so must the Son of Man be lifted up . . ." (John 3:14). Jesus also enters Jerusalem for his fateful last week on the back of a colt.

But these images are again balanced by equally negative ones of the relationship between humans and the animals. In Matthew 10 Jesus admonishes his listeners about worrying, arguing that not a single sparrow falls to the ground without God's knowledge. "So do not be afraid," Jesus continues, "you are of more value than many sparrows" (Matthew 10:31). And despite the usually positive association we have of the wild animals being with Jesus in the wilderness, in biblical days wild animals were more often understood as dangerous and deadly; some scholars argue that the image of Jesus in the wilderness is not a pastoral image at all. These images, and others, reflect the early belief that humans matter more to God than animals do.

Even so, there are also sections of the Christian testament that imply God's love and care for all of creation, even when the animals are not named specifically. The most persuasive and clear one for me has been this one from Colossians 1, which speaks of the reconciliation of the entire created order in the new covenant ushered in with Jesus.

> He [Jesus] is the image of the invisible God, the firstborn of all creation; for in him all things in heaven and on earth were created, things visible and invisible, whether thrones or dominions or rulers or powers—all things have been created through him and for him. He himself is before all things, and in him all things hold together. . . . For in him all the fullness of God was pleased to dwell, and through him God was pleased to reconcile to himself all things, whether on earth or in heaven, by making peace through the blood of his cross. And you, who were once estranged and hostile in mind . . . he has now reconciled in his fleshly body . . . provided that you continue securely established and steadfast in the faith . . . which has been proclaimed to every creature under heaven."
>
> —Colossians 1:15–23

Interpreting this passage, Paulos Mar Gregorios, who was the Metropolitan of Delhi in the Indian Orthodox Church, writes that

Christ "assumed flesh. . . . He took matter into himself, so matter is not alien to him now. His body is a material body—transformed, of course, but transformed matter. Thus he shares his being with the whole created order: animals and birds, snakes and worms, flowers and seeds. All parts of creation are now reconciled in Christ. And the created order is to be set free and to share in the glorious freedom of the children of God."[12]

The ancient Celts expressed similar understandings in their poetry, prayers, and stories. As Celtic scholar A.M. Allchin notes, for the Celts "Christ is the Word by whom all things were made. In his death and resurrection, all things were changed because he is the one in whom all things hold together from the beginning. . . . [B]y the resurrection of Christ the whole destiny of the world is made manifest."[13]

Taken as a whole the various references to animals in the Bible leave us without a clear picture. Scholars have spent lots of energy dissecting these passages, looking at the texts in their original language or early translations, trying to understand not only what individual words or phrases mean, but whether or not the use of the word or phrase in a particular context is positive or negative. As with so many issues, various passages from the Bible can be used to argue for or against a given perspective, much as we used the Bible to justify slavery or the subjugation of women in the past. The passages clearly exist in our most sacred text which argue that God gave humans the right to use animals in any way they wish, or to argue the opposite—that God loves the animals as deeply as anything else God created, and that we are asked to give them loving care.

From my own perspective, I believe the time has come for a shift in the way we have traditionally read many of these texts, the same kind of shift that has happened repeatedly in our history. At one point in history, for instance, we believed that our own earth was the center of all that existed, that all of the planets and stars revolved around us. In 1543 Nicolas Copernicus argued that the sun was actually the center of our universe, not the earth, a theory that rocked the scientific and religious world. I hope that we are ready for a shift in our thinking again, moving away from understanding ourselves as the center of God's interest, and imagining ourselves and all that was created, including the animals, metaphorically revolving around God.

My own sense is that God is much bigger than most of us can imagine, and perhaps this causes us to imagine God with limitations. I don't believe that God created all that exists, and carefully saved all of it before the Flood, but then had a change of heart, and only saved people in the new covenant. I wonder, sometimes, if we're simply afraid that God's love isn't big enough to love all of creation, that the God we imagine is too small. I don't know if humans are more important than animals, or if all that was created by God is equal in God's heart, and I don't expect to have an answer to that on this side of the grave. Arguing that the Bible is an accurate reflection of God's hopes for humans, and using God's argument to Job that Job wasn't there at the beginning of creation and did not know God's mind, John Burnaby, who was a professor of divinity at the University of Cambridge, wrote:

The purposes of creation as a whole must be beyond our comprehension. But we can believe that God, in revealing himself in Christ, has therewith shown us his purpose *"for us men"*—what man is meant to be. And this should make it impossible for us to think that God has created all things with no other purpose than the satisfaction of men's natural desires and needs. We need not abandon the ancient insight, whereby the purpose of man's being, that in which he is to find his fulfillment, is embraced in the purpose of all creation—the *glory* of God. The glory of God in the Bible and Christian tradition has always been linked with the idea of light. The light of the sun enables those who have eyes to see the world lit up with splendor. God is glorified on earth when the eyes of men are enlightened, when they see his goodness in his works and come to worship him. But it would be presumptuous to imagine that the glory of God *depends* on the existence of the human eye. [14]

I believe that Dr. Burnaby is correct: We cannot fully know what is in God's mind and heart. The best we can do is to continue to try to refine our own sense of it through reading Scripture, through prayer, and through our own experience of the world around us. And in doing these things we will, perhaps, come to understand that God's hopes and desires for the world are larger than we may have previously understood. In terms of the way I live with animals, this means that I try to show as much respect and compassion as I can to all living beings, and avoid gratuitous violence toward them. In practical terms this means that I'm okay with drowning the fleas I find on my cat, but I'm more comfortable with giving the cats monthly flea medicine that prevents fleas from feasting on them in the first place.

Can we, as contemporary churches have done with Paul's words about women, recognize that our sacred texts were written centuries ago, and that these words need to be continually examined in light of our best understanding of God today? Most of us no longer believe that women should be subjects of their husbands or their fathers, or that slavery is appropriate. Can we also perhaps acknowledge that we have placed ourselves ahead of the animals in God's estimation, and this may not have been what God actually intended? Can we entertain the idea that all creation is meant to be redeemed and saved, not just people?

Miriam Therese Winter recently said that:

[W]e need a new lens that refracts a wider and more empathetic understanding of the world in which we live, one that will bring into sharper focus the Spirit-led role we are to play in an ever-expanding universe. We can see to the edge of the universe now but remain strangely captivated by a world of our own making. Yet we must look beyond it, look long and hard into our own souls for the soft underbelly of mercy, face the dividing lines of our differences, the restrictions of religiosity, the confines of our canons, the precipice of our prejudices, and dare to step across the chasm to experience the other side. That is what Jesus did.[15]

Winter was not writing about animals, but when we truly see from the perspective of the other, and play a Spirit-led role in the universe, this includes, for me, acknowledging that the animals are creatures of God, just as we are, ones who deserve to be treated with God-like respect, compassion, and love.

My own sense is that the Bible as a whole calls us to live compassionate lives, that we are called to be loving beings, and to care for all that exists—animate and inanimate. Perhaps Christian poet Christina Rossetti was right, and that all that exists has "just as good a right to its appointed portion of delight."

And other eyes than ours
Were made to look on flowers,
Eyes of small birds and insects small:
The deep sun-blushing rose
Round which the prickles close
Opens her bosom to them all.
The tiniest living thing
That soars on feathered wing,
Or crawls among the long grass out of sight
Has just as good a right
To its appointed portion of delight
As any King.

—Christina Rossetti

This book is about providing the animals that live with us in our homes—domestic animals—with their "appointed portion of delight," and about discovering God's presence through and in the midst of our relationships with them. The dogs, cats, guinea pigs, gerbils, birds, and other creatures who live in our homes provide us with opportunities for Christian practice, for deepening our relationship with the whole of God's creation. Bringing a new animal into the house is an opportunity to practice hospitality. Caring for the daily needs of these companions helps us exercise the Benedictine practices of stability and obedience. Caring for a sick animal teaches compassion. Above all, perhaps, living with an animal teaches us what it means to covenant with another living being, and to live out that covenant. As Church historian Roberta Bondi writes, based on her own experiences of living with cats:

> Like our relationship with God, our relationships to the animals with whom we live is a deep and wonderful mystery. They are like us and at the same time utterly unlike us. They teach us compassion for our own kind. They also, like God's own self, show us how to love across species in a way that is "homely," to use Julian of Norwich's word, and paradoxically beyond all power to understand it. Such love and mystery fills us with awe, as well as a sense of the presence of beauty beyond anything we can imagine. It makes us humble; it teaches us gentleness; it opens us to joy. [16]

Animals, like many other aspects of creation, point us back to God. They can show us aspects of God and God's creation that we might not learn from humans alone.

There are many people and groups in the world today who are working not only on caring for the animals, but on issues of animal rights and welfare. How we treat animals we use for food, medical testing, or just for sport, is an important and complicated issue today. But if we are just beginning to think about our relationship to the animals as a part of creation it may be best to start with what we can wrap our minds around most easily. Some may not be ready to consider that animals have rights, and what the implications of our covenant with animals may be as far as the food we eat, our sporting activities, and a variety of other culturally sanctioned ways of treating those whom early Christians and others refer to as our brothers and sisters. Those questions seem too large, too abstract, and the powers that sanction these activities too entrenched for any one of us to make any difference. But we can expand our understandings by starting with the animals we live with, by recognizing the love we have for them, and what the covenant we make with them means in everyday life.

For some of us, God willing, coming to know the cat who lives with us as one of God's beloved creatures will lead to loving even more of the animals who walk on the earth with us, and recognizing them as truly our brothers and sisters. Living with any animal, and coming to know its wants, needs, and ways teaches us respect and awe for the Other. And, if we are open and receptive to the animals who live with us, we will find ourselves being ministered to, and taught by them as well.

Why Should We Care?

While the care of and concern for any part of God's creation is good and holy in and of itself, there is evidence that learning to care for the animals is also good for us. They draw us away from self-absorption, and help us become more compassionate people.

In a northern California community a large prison and the local Humane Society match prisoners with dogs who aren't adoptable for health or sociability reasons. Two prisoners are assigned to one dog, and live with it and provide 24/7 care, whether that be nursing care or just practice in being more sociable. The dogs become adoptable and easier to match with a permanent family or individual. The prison's warden, and even the prisoners themselves, affirm that the need to pay attention to the dogs' needs encourages the practice of compassion, and draws prisoners away from focusing exclusively on themselves—something that happens easily in prison environments.[17]

A similar program, "Project Pooch," matches young juvenile offenders with rescued dogs that are considered un-adoptable. In the process of training his dog, each young man discovers the power of persistence, patience, and attention. Each teen learns to be responsible for his dog, and in return, many of them have their own first experience of unconditional love. Since the program's inception in 1993, none of the Project Pooch youths have entered juvenile detention again.[18]

What is true for these prisoners is true for the rest of us as well. Animals draw us out of ourselves, and away from our own agendas and our self-absorption. It's very difficult to stay focused on our anger over some silly slight when the cat jumps on your lap and starts purring furiously, when the dog—tail wagging—approaches with a rubber ball in her mouth, or when the gerbil in her plastic bubble rolls over our bare foot.

There is also a great deal of evidence that animals can be part of healing for human beings. Retirement communities, which used to forbid the presence of domestic animals, thereby adding the loss of a beloved animal to the loss of independence for new members, are rethinking those policies and allowing people to bring beloved animals along with them. Nursing homes and other therapeutic environments bring in specially trained dogs and cats to connect with patients, some of whom respond to little else. Our local library, like others in the country, helps children who find reading difficult, and who read well below their grade levels, by pairing them with a dog. The children read out aloud to their dogs, and their reading levels improve quickly and substantially. The children know that the dogs don't care if they make mistakes, and so the children's self-confidence grows.

Animals are, at least in some sense, our brothers and sisters; they were created out of the same dust from which we were created. They care about and love us. When we hurt them—when we hurt any part of creation—we hurt ourselves. In our industrial age we have been slow to learn this; we've treated the earth itself with the same callousness with which we often treat animals. But the ways in which we have damaged the earth have begun to catch up with us, and we're beginning to discover that we really are all truly interrelated. To damage one piece of that creation damages the whole. To think that we are lords and masters of all, and can do whatever we wish without considering the consequences of our actions, not only risks the destruction of creation itself, but is damaging to our own souls. Archbishop Desmond Tutu speaks of this interrelationship with inanimate things, but I believe it also applies to our relationships with the animals:

> The world is also discovering we were made for interdependence not just with human beings; we are finding out that we depend on what used to be called inanimate nature. When Africans said, "Oh, don't treat that tree like that, it feels pain," others used to say, "Ah, they're prescientific, they're primitive." It is wonderful now how we are beginning to discover that it is true—that that tree does hurt, and if you hurt the tree, in an extraordinary way you hurt yourself. . . .
>
> The Bible also tells us of our relationship to the rest of creation and the sacredness of God's creation, all of it in its glory and physicality. We are stewards of all this, and so it is not to be involved in a passing fad to be concerned about the environment, about ecology. It is not just being politically correct to be green. The material universe has a high density. The dominion

we were given in Genesis 1:26 was so that we should rule as God's viceroys, doing it as God would—caringly, gently, not harshly or exploitatively, with a deep reverence, for all is ultimately holy ground, and we should figuratively take off our shoes, for it all has the potential to be "theophanic"—to reveal the divine. Every shrub has the ability to be a burning bush and to offer us an encounter with the transcendent.[19]

Every shrub may turn out to be a burning bush, and every animal we meet may be our teacher.

Finally, to love and care for animals is an indescribable joy. There are many theological and moral reasons to protect the animals, but from a purely selfish perspective, most of the time our domestic animals love us back, or at least that's what those of us who live with animals, feel. We may not be able to know what's in the mind of an animal any more than we do with God's mind, but each species of domestic animal has characteristics that humans find loveable and life-giving. How joyful it is to play fetch with a willing dog, or to listen to the deep purr of a contented cat. I spent one perfectly delightful afternoon enjoying the antics of a bird who couldn't bear a messy environment, and she spent the entire afternoon attacking mess with more persistence than I've ever been able to manage in cleaning. The sheer joy with which animals play brings hours of delight and laughter into our lives.

Animals are sources of solace as well. Many is the time that a cat or dog cuddling up with me has provided comfort or brought peace to my day. There have even been cases where animals have been the rescuers for humans, even in ways that seem to us selfless. In the town in which I live a dog recently alerted the sleeping humans with whom he lived of a fire in the house. Since they didn't have a smoke alarm they may well have died had the dog not barked insistently and forced them out of their beds.

How we care for and nurture the animals we live with is not only good for the animal, but good for our own souls. This is not, however, a book about how to take care of your pet's nutrition, health care, and social needs per se. I'm not a veterinarian, and I leave advice on all such matters to those who know them best. While I'll provide some basic guidelines about the kind of care animals need, this is not a substitute for the information your own veterinarian can provide about your specific animal. This is a book for approaching the care of your pets from a spiritual perspective, in a way that acknowledges that when we bring animals into our homes we have made a covenant with them, one that involves great joy but also gives us an obligation and a responsibility. That may sound rather abstract, but there are practical ways of living in godly relationship with animals.

If you already live with a companion animal you're probably already offering them some of the care suggested: You're feeding, training, and playing with the animal. What I'd like to suggest to you is that you care for your companion in an intentionally Christian way, that you look at the care you provide for your friend through a Christian lens. In each of the chapters that follow I'll provide some background about the various opportunities to provide a domestic animal with Christian care, as well as practices, prayers, and rituals that may be helpful for individuals and families. The prayers provided don't need to be memorized or used on any regular basis; think of them more as starters to your own prayers. In a previous book (*Unceasing Prayer*) I talked about the ways in which the tasks we do and the conversations we have each day can spur us to remember that God is present in every moment and every interaction. We can ask God, for instance, to clean our hearts (Psalm 51) as we clean our bodies each morning. Use the prayers and rituals provided here in the same way, as starting places for your own way of acknowledging God's presence in the relationship you have with your companion. Don't feel that you need to use all of them, but I encourage you to try some of the practices, even if you're not quite sure how you feel about them. Sometimes it is in trying the practices themselves that we come to understand their meaning and the theological and ethical perspectives that inform them.

A Few Words about Words

A few words about language in this book are necessary here. The first is that the word "animals" is itself problematic, since humans are animals as well. Some writers have dealt with this issue by using the term "non-human animals," but that's pretty cumbersome in a book that isn't intended for biologists or theologians. When I use the word "animals" in this book, it is with the knowledge that humans are animals as well, but I'm using it here to refer to the domestic non-human animals that we live with.

It is also difficult, in today's world, to find the right pronouns for writing about animals. Most writers refer to animals as an "it," just as they would write about a chair or a book. I find the use of "it" for an animal to be distasteful and disrespectful; the word distances us from the mutuality involved in living with another being that deserves as much respect as each human being does. For the most part, I will avoid the use of "it" when referring to our companions, but given the constraints of the English language, that usage cannot always be avoided. I've made every attempt to speak of animals in other ways, and ask the reader's forgiveness when that hasn't been possible.

You will also quickly notice that I'm avoiding the use of the words "pet" and "owner." While there's nothing wrong with the word "pet" in general, too often it has come to imply something inferior, as in: "It's just a pet." I do use the word "pet" for the physical action of stroking an animal, but when I'm speaking of the animal directly, I use words such as "animal companion" and others that, I hope, denote a greater respect for the animals we live with. The word "owner" is avoided at all costs. We do not *own* the animals we invite into our homes; they are first guests, and then members of the family. We do not own them any more than we own our children, and our covenant with and responsibility for them arise out of mutual respect and love, not out of lordship over an inferior creature.

The cat that jumped in my lap during morning prayers those years ago is now a blessed memory, but as I began to write this book I was caring for a group of three kittens who have now grown into fine adult cats. One of them, Lily, jumped in my lap one morning while I sat in my chair and said morning prayers. She joins me every morning now, leaping into my lap the minute I sit down and take up my prayer book. She is, for me, a symbol of the sacred, creative, and loving energy of God, one that sits on me and purrs. So morning prayers are said with Lily each day, holding a prayer book in one hand, and petting her with the other. "Come, Lord Jesus," I pray now, "and feel free to sit in my lap."

O God, enlarge within us the sense of fellowship with all living things, our brothers the animals to whom thou gavest the earth as their home in common with us.

We remember with shame that in the past we have exercised the high dominion of man with ruthless cruelty so that the voice of the earth, which should have gone up to thee in song, has been a groan of travail. May we realize that they live not for us alone but for themselves and for thee, and that they love the sweetness of life.

—St. Basil

CHAPTER ONE

Covenant and Commitment

❧❧❧❧

*I will make for you a covenant on that day with the wild animals, the
birds of the air, and the creeping things of the ground.* —Hosea 2:18

*I*t wasn't quite like the Inquisition, but the shelter did mean
business. The first time I adopted a cat from the shelter they
handed me several forms to fill out. One of those forms was
a long list of questions pertaining to my fitness to care for an animal.
What's your income? How much do you anticipate care of your animal will cost each year? How many hours will the animal be home
alone each day? Have you ever lived with an animal before? Do you
own or rent your home, and, if you rent, are animals permitted in
your dwelling? What would you do with your dog or cat if you had
to move to a place where animals aren't permitted? And the question
that no one probably wanted to answer in the affirmative: Have you
ever given an animal away before?

I don't remember all the questions asked on those forms, but the shelter was making a good point. Adopting an animal is serious business,

and the shelter wants to make sure you've thought it through before they let you take a dog or cat home with you.

Though shelters don't ask their questions out of a specifically spiritual perspective, these are still spiritual questions for us. They relate to a covenant we are considering making, a promise or vow that we take when we choose to bring an animal into our lives. A covenant, often referred to in biblical texts, involves an agreement between two parties about how they will interact with each other. With an animal we can't get the verbal or written agreement of both parties, any more than we can with a child we hope to bring into the world, but we do commit ourselves to the care and support of that animal. We are making a commitment about our own future conduct, knowing that some days it will be easy to walk the dog, but that we'll have to do it even when the temperature outside is 10 degrees and the wind chill makes it feel even worse.

A friend of mine has a cat who gave him a good bit of trouble at one point. The cat constantly urinated around one of his windows. After trying everything he could think of he seriously considered euthanizing the cat, but finally realized that he didn't have the right to do that. He'd made a covenant with this animal when he brought him into his home. He later discovered that neighborhood cats were congregating outside the window where his cat was urinating and his cat, as cats will do, was clearly marking her territory. Once the source of the problem was revealed, however, he was able to prevent future occurrences. Part of his covenant to care for his cat was finding and solving the source of the problem if possible, rather than treating the cat as expendable.

Various animal shelters have had a lot of experience with people who haven't carefully considered the commitment they're making to an animal. All too often cats and dogs are simply discarded as if they weren't worth a second thought. But our ancestors, the Celts, who felt a deep reverence for animals, tell stories to remind us that animals are worthy of our care and concern. St. Kevin, one of the Celtic saints, was praying in his hermitage one Lent. Kneeling on the floor, he stretched his arms out, lifting them to heaven; one of his arms extended out through his window. As he prayed (and it must have been a long prayer session!) a blackbird settled on his hand, built a nest on it, and laid an egg in the nest. Kevin, so moved with the bird's trust of him, left his hand outstretched until the egg hatched and the mother and baby bird flew away.

Few of us could equal Kevin's commitment to the blackbird and her baby, but his story illuminates the seriousness of the kind of covenant we need to make with an animal. If you've lived with an animal before, you probably have some idea about the kind of care and nurture that's required. I remember my own feeling of anxiety the first time I was responsible for a cat's care. I grew up with lots of cats and dogs, as well as smaller animals, in our home, so I thought I knew all about their care. But living with a cat as an adult—when

I was responsible for knowing what needed to be done, or even whether the cat was healthy or sick—was a whole different matter.

Codi, the first cat I had as an adult, was always a little sickly. He hadn't been healthy as a kitten, and he continued to have some minor health problems during his first few years. I suspect I was a little like a mother with her first child, and that I was overly watchful for any little sign of illness or distress. One day Codi seemed to be breathing oddly to me. My next door neighbor at the time was not only seasoned in animal care, but a registered nurse as well, so I went to her for help. She came over, sat next to Codi, petted him for a few moments, and listened to him breathing. "Codi's fine," she finally said to me, "but you're not doing so well. Come on over to my house for a while, watch the Olympics on television, and leave Codi to rest for a bit." She was right, Codi was fine, but it took time for me to relax and find the right balance between vigilance to Codi's needs, and letting him just be a cat.

If you've never lived with an animal, or not been the person responsible for his care, a little advance research is in order. There are lots of books on the market detailing the care and training of almost any animal that might commonly be found in a home. Veterinarians are often excellent sources of both information and referrals. If you're looking for a purebred cat or dog talk to various breeders about the characteristics of the kind of animal you're considering and find out if that animal is a good match for your situation. Talk to others who live with animals and find out what they love about animal care and nurture, and what they find more tedious.

If you're expecting a child to help with the care of an animal, help your child learn about the covenant he or she is about to make as well. A friend of mine took her daughter to visit three local vets to learn about the care of her new dog. Two of the vets ignored the girl, while the third sat down with her and asked her questions about how she was going to feed the dog, what she was going to do if the dog was sick, and so on. My friend's daughter learned a lot about the care of her dog, and also about the expectations of her parents in relation to the promises she was making to her dog, and about everyone's confidence that she was ready for such an important responsibility.

The covenant made with an animal is never one to take lightly. It's easy to accept the love of an affectionate cat or dog or other domestic animal, but they need to be loved in return. You are covenanting with an animal to provide that love, not only with pats here and there, but with attention in the wee hours of the night if need be, with a suitable physical environment for the animal to live in, with appropriate food, training, and veterinary care.

Perhaps most important to the whole process of consideration of adding an animal to your home is your sense of what God is calling you to do. Do you feel called to care for an animal? Do you feel called to raise one from the beginning of her life or to rescue an animal who needs a good home? Maybe a dear friend or relative has died and left behind an animal who needs care. Many people feel called to care for animals, such as greyhounds, who would otherwise be discarded when they are no longer able to perform at adequate racing levels. Others care for wild birds, bats, and even sick or injured marine animals. A friend of mine finds great satisfaction in helping to socialize feral (wild) kittens who have been trapped and caught, so the cats can be adopted into good homes. There are many different callings when it comes to bringing an animal into your home, all of them noble.

St. Ignatius, who lived in the sixteenth century, developed a strategy for discerning God's calling for an individual in his *Spiritual Exercises*. I doubt that he intended it to be used to discover what your own calling is in terms of animal companionship, but his system is so useful that I'm going to suggest a modified version of it to you.

Ignatius begins by reminding us to be clear about the decision in front of us. "The first point," he writes, "is to put before myself the matter about which I wish to make an election."[20] (An election, for Ignatius, is what we would call a decision.) This sounds simple, but may be more complex than you realize. You might discover, for instance, that you're feeling lonely and that's why you want to bring an animal in the house. In this case, the question might be more about how to handle your loneliness, than about whether or not to find an animal companion.

Focus on the question of whether or not you are called to care for an animal, and try to remain open to whatever answer you sense coming from God, even if that answer is no. Again, Ignatius is the good advisor: "It is necessary to keep as my objective the end for which I am created, to praise God our Lord and save my soul. Furthermore, I ought to find myself indifferent, that is, without any disordered affection, to such an extent that I am not more inclined or emotionally disposed toward taking the matter proposed rather than letting go if it, nor more toward letting it go rather than taking it."

Finally, in preparation, Ignatius reminds us that we should each ask God to "move my will and to put into my mind what I ought to do." Ignatius then asks us to engage both our reason and also our imagination in considering the decision in front of us. Over a series of days, or longer if need be, try the following.

Make a list of pros and cons about having an animal in your life. What will be gained and lost if you decide to bring an animal into your home? What would be gained or lost if you decided not to add an animal to your home right now? Be honest with your answers. You don't need to show these lists to anyone, and God already knows what the pros and cons are, so there's nothing to lose in being honest here.

Once the list is complete Ignatius asks us to consider "to which side reason more inclines." My sense of what is reasonable, however, may be different from yours. In addition I would suggest that when you have finished, consider how these lists feel to you. Do you feel yourself more or less drawn to an option? Does this help at all in sensing what is more reasonable? You may have ten answers in one column and one in the other, but the shorter column may still be the more reasonable and compelling, so don't go by the numbers; pay attention to which option brings with it more energy and perhaps a sense of rightness. Once we have a sense of what is most reasonable, we should present that option to God in prayer.

Next, Ignatius asks us to look to our imagination for an answer, and he suggests several ways of doing this. First, imagine a friend of yours in your same situation, and think about what advice you would give to her. That may well be the advice you should take yourself. Second, imagine that you are at the end of your life and running back through all that you've done with God. How would you feel about having or not having had animals in your life? When I give workshops on discernment and use Ignatius's *Spiritual Exercises*, I sometimes suggest to people that they write their obituary. What would you like your obituary to say about you and the animals?

Finally, imagine yourself on Judgment Day, explaining your decisions to God. "Imagining and considering in what condition I find myself on judgment day," Ignatius writes, "I will think how at that time I will wish I had decided in regard to the present matter." The image of Judgment Day may seem overly harsh to some contemporary readers, and if that's true for you, just imagine yourself on the other side of the grave in conversation with God about your life. What would you want to be able to say?

After doing these exercises, Ignatius suggests we look again at what seems most reasonable, and present that to God in prayer. Ignatius suggests that we use both of these practices—the reason and the imagination—as ways of listening for God's guidance. If they are both pointing you in the same direction, you are most likely hearing clearly. If others confirm what you are sensing from God as well, that's even better.

If you sense that it is time for an animal companion, take a little quiet time to write a covenant with the animal you hope to find. This doesn't need to be a long and detailed document; just a few sentences will do. What is the promise that you're making to your animal? This could be something quite simple such as: "As I think about and joyfully anticipate the gift of an animal companion in my life, I promise to love and care for him/her with food and water, with health care, with a safe and comfortable place to live, and through time spent playing with and comforting her (him) for the length of her (his) life." Write it down, and place it somewhere where you'll see it on a regular basis. Try to anticipate, very concretely, what living this covenant out will be like in your household. You won't be able to completely understand it, of course, until you actually bring the particular animal into your home. A friend of mine brought a dog home, and after several months of living with the dog, he and his family realized that he was not a good fit for the household. They kept their covenant with the dog, however, by finding him an excellent home.

As you continue to anticipate the addition of an animal to the household, include the following prayer in your own daily prayers as a reminder of the sacredness of what you are considering:

Most high and most glorious God,
enlighten the darkness of my heart and give me truer faith,
more certain hope, and perfect charity, sense and knowledge of you,
so that I may carry out your holy and true command for my life.
—St. Francis of Assisi[21]

CHAPTER TWO
Preparing a Place

The LORD appeared to Abraham by the oaks of Mamre, as he sat at the entrance of his tent in the heat of the day. He looked up and saw three men standing near him. When he saw them, he ran from the tent entrance to meet them, and bowed down to the ground. He said, "My lord, if I find favor with you, do not pass by your servant. Let a little water be brought, and wash your feet, and rest yourselves under the tree. Let me bring a little bread, that you may refresh yourselves."   —Genesis 18:1–5

*W*hen my travels take me to New York City, I usually stay at an Episcopal convent. The sisters provide a simple but welcoming place for travelers, and those of us staying there may join them for worship and for meals as we wish. Convents and monasteries set up the spaces for visitors carefully, providing what is necessary for basic comfort. The space is a simple one—a bed, some light to see and read by, sometimes a dresser and a desk to write at, sometimes a simple but comfortable chair. Whatever is provided is put there with care and forethought so that visitors know they're welcome. Before we leave we are asked to help make the space welcoming for the next guest by changing the bed sheets. The sisters even provide a prayer for stripping and re-making the bed, one that reminds us that our task is a sacred one.

The practice of hospitality goes back to biblical times, and is found throughout the Hebrew Scriptures and the New Testament. "In the ancient Near East," biblical scholar Bruce Malina writes, "hospitality was the process of 'receiving' outsiders and changing them from strangers to guests."[22] As the nuns open up their space and welcome visitors in ways that change them from strangers to guests, so too can we prepare places of hospitality to help new animals move from being strangers in our homes to guests, and finally to members of the family. (It is difficult, of course, to actually create a space for an animal if you don't know what animal will be coming home with you, so read this chapter and the next, on picking the right animal for you, in whatever order makes sense to you.)

Not too long ago I adopted three kittens who had been fostered by a friend who volunteers at a local shelter. The kittens, all siblings, had respiratory problems, and had been separated from the rest of the shelter population so they could recover. My friend had kept the kittens at her own home, on behalf of the shelter, for almost two months. When they were well enough to go to a new home, I adopted them and brought them to my home, which I thought I had prepared carefully.

I had an adult cat already, and had set up a space for the kittens to keep them isolated from my adult cat until I was sure the kittens were completely healthy. I had filled the room with inexpensive toys that kittens love, as well as climbing and scratching posts. I'd kitten-proofed the room to make sure they couldn't destroy anything, or get tangled or caught in anything, and that nothing would fall and hurt them. Their food and litter dishes were handy. There was plenty of space for running around.

What I discovered, however, was that there was too much space for the small kittens. As usually happens with kittens and cats, they were terrified of the new people and environment, and had too few places to hide. I hadn't planned on the necessity of medicating them twice a day, so that when they did hide in the few places available to them, I had no way of getting them out. The space, which was meant to be a hospitable environment for three recovering kittens, didn't work at all. I quickly transformed a smaller room in my home—one with nooks and crannies to hide in but no big furniture to cower under—into the kitten's infirmary for the next few weeks. It was the perfect space. The kittens could hide when they needed to, and they could run around and wrestle. I could sit on the floor in the room and let them come to me when they were brave enough to check me out. There were soft sleeping spaces, and two windows to look out. The room became the perfect sanctuary space for the kittens until they were well enough to meet their adult housemate.

Sometimes figuring out what needs to be done to make a welcoming environment for the newest member of the household requires research. A friend of mine who decided that her ministry with animals should center on taking in rescue dogs—ones that had been mistreated or abandoned—spent time reading about how to make them welcome, and specifically how to provide an environment that felt safe and secure. Rescue animals often have very specific problems and needs, and she was wise to learn about those in advance, rather than being completely surprised by them later. Local veterinarians, as well as the staff at local pet stores and animal shelters, are all good resources for learning about the best environment to set up for the animal you're considering adding to your home. They can also direct you to books that may be helpful. This kind of research is a further way of making sure—in a very concrete way—that you are actually called to care for an animal, and that you have the capacity to do so.

This kind of welcome is well grounded in Christian tradition. All monasteries have rules or guidelines for welcoming visitors. The most famous rule, the sixth-century one from St. Benedict, reminds the monks to provide guests with water for washing, food, and adequate bedding, among other things. Benedict's rule harks back to biblical days when providing hospitality to strangers included washing the dust off the guest's feet, and providing food and water not only for the guest(s) but any animals they might have with them. Washing the dust off a gerbil's feet probably isn't a good idea, but we can still plan an animal's environment with some of the biblical and monastic understandings of hospitality in mind. As you begin to plan to bring an animal companion home, plan her space intentionally with the knowledge that your task is sacred, just as is making the beds in the monastery. Some of the things to think about when extending hospitality to an animal might include:

- The animal's nutritional needs.
- Sleeping areas and materials.
- Playing areas and equipment when needed.
- Safety issues, pet-proofing when required, and making sure that the animal will be safe from any environmental hazards (such as cleaning materials, poisons, plants, and so on.) The safety issues will vary by animal; your local veterinarian can be helpful here.
- Secure areas for the animal, ones that are secure from other animals in the house, at least at the beginning, and places where the animal can go to feel secure and safe.
- Something for carrying the animal to this space, and later, to vet appointments, safely.
- A veterinarian. Be sure you have a relationship with a local veterinarian before selecting, or at least bringing home, an animal.

None of this needs to entail spending a fortune. You may need to purchase some items, such as habitats, crates, carrying cases, and other such items if you've never lived with an animal before. Purchasing food, and perhaps some toys, will also be necessary. If you've got the skills, you might even want to make a bed or toys for your friend. But there's no need to overspend on setting up a hospitable environment. My cats consistently like the inexpensive and free toys—like string—much more than any of the expensive gadgets I used to buy them. As the monks and nuns do, set up living quarters that take care of the basic needs and provide for the animal's comfort and safety, but don't feel as if the more you spend the happier the animal will be. Beyond the basics listed above, your love is what your companion needs most.

When the space is ready, take a few moments to bless the space. If you've set up a room for the animal, stand in that space along with any other members of the household who want to participate. Otherwise stand near, and perhaps place your hands on, some object that will be for the animal's comfort and care. This can be a food dish, a habitat or enclosure of some sort, a blanket, or anything else the animal will use. Speak a prayer of your own, or use the following prayer to bless these objects and/or the space. Say the prayer out loud; if you have a group gathered, consider having part of the group speak the first two lines, and the other part the second two lines, and so on.

Lord our God,
may Your divine name be always holy within our home.
May You, as Holy Father and Divine Mother,
lovingly care for all who shall live here.

May Your kingdom come in this home
as we love and respect one another.
May we always do Your holy will
by living in harmony and unity.

Amen.

—Edward Hays[23]

CHAPTER THREE
Choosing Wisely

O send out your light and your truth; let them lead me.
—Psalm 43:3

Last winter I took a class at our local botanical gardens. The gardening columnist from our local paper was the presenter in this class for beginning gardeners. "Most new gardeners go to the plant nursery," he told us, "and they look around and they bring home every plant they like. They don't worry too much about whether or not they have a place to put it where it will flourish. They like the color or the design, and they bring it home." "Busted," I thought to myself. That's exactly what I'd done just the year before—which is why I was taking the class. Some of the plants that I'd purchased did fine; some didn't. But it was clear to me that a little planning and foresight was in order.

The same is true when you're going out to find an animal to bring into your home. Every year around Christmas the news channels run features about thinking twice about surprising someone with a kitten or a puppy for Christmas. When I was a child the local pharmacy used to sell baby chicks or bunnies at Easter, a practice that probably led to many animal deaths at the hands of well-meaning people. While the intention is good, too often people don't think carefully about whether or not the recipient is old enough (in the case of a child) for a companion animal, or whether the recipient can care for the animal adequately. It's easy to fall in love with an animal—especially a young one—but raising a kitten or puppy or bunny or a baby chick requires a lot more care than does a daffodil. Just as it is important to discern whether you are called to care for an animal companion, discerning what kind of animal you can provide for is part of our ethical obligation to these other creatures of God.

The Right Match

Plants need a regular watering, and maybe some plant food occasionally, but animals require daily care and companionship. They need food and water, a safe environment, someone to care for their health needs, and someone to pet them and play with them. If you've never lived with an animal before, do a little research or talk to your local veterinarian and find out whether the care and attention required by a given kind of animal fits with your own environment and schedule. It's so easy, and even noble, to fall in love with animals who need someone to care for them, but bringing an animal into our home that we don't actually have the capacity to care for isn't a good way to practice compassion. And so the very practical questions around selecting the right animal for your home are actually ethical ones as well; you're looking for an animal that you are capable of caring for just as God would.

Some animals require less constant attention, while others thrive with quite a bit of interaction. How often are you or other family members home to care for the animal? What kind of living quarters can you provide for the animal? Will it need to be an indoor or outdoor animal, or some combination of both? Does anyone in the house have allergies that will affect what kind of animal you invite in? Are there young children in the house who might affect the kind of animal you select? Are there other animals already in the house who will need to adjust to a new companion? Who will care for the animal when you're away on vacation? Is there a particular sized animal, or a temperament, that will fit best in your life? Some friends of mine, for instance, wanted a small dog that they could travel with, and looked for a dog that was small enough and had a gentle temperament so they could bring him on airplanes with them.

In addition to these fundamental questions, it's worth asking yourself (and any other primary caregivers) what kind of time and attention you're willing to provide. Are you willing to work, perhaps for weeks or months, with an animal who might need a lot of socialization before she's comfortable and friendly? Are you looking for an animal who will most likely be low-maintenance, or do you have the time, patience, and perhaps financial resources, to care for an animal that has special needs? Do you have the energy required to raise a young animal—particularly a puppy or kitten—or would an adult animal that's already trained be more suitable in your home? There are no right or wrong answers to these questions. Each of us has different gifts and abilities, and it isn't fair—either to ourselves or to the animal—to try to be someone we're not. Think carefully about what kind of animal fits into your home and lifestyle; that way you'll make a good choice of an animal whose needs you are truly prepared to meet.

Another question to be considered when you're thinking about bringing an animal into your home is whether or not it is ethical to bring that specific kind of animal into your home, or into any domestic environment. There are no end of exotic animals available these days, but they are not always—perhaps ever—appropriate for a domestic environment. In a story about St. Francis, commonly considered the patron saint of animals, Francis rescued a cage full of turtledoves that had been captured by a young man. Francis felt sorry for the birds, and begged the boy to give the birds to him. "I pray that you will give them to me, these birds that are so gentle, which holy scripture compares to chaste, humble, and faithful souls, so that they will not fall into the hands of cruel people intent on killing them."[24] The young man gave Francis the birds, and Francis created nests for them and kept them at the monastery. But realizing, perhaps, that the birds did not belong at the monastery, Francis and his brothers eventually freed the birds, and they returned to their home in the country.

This story of capturing exotic animals and keeping them in environments where they do not belong continues today. When I was in Austin recently the evening news featured a story about all the exotic animals (snakes, lizards, large cats, and others) being brought over the border illegally and sold, only to be abandoned by people who couldn't actually care for them. The Austin zoo could barely make space for the large cats surrendered to them, and was having to find other homes for these animals who were trapped, and often maimed in some way so that they could never be returned to the wild. Even organizations that work with animals are realizing that some animals simply shouldn't be penned up; a variety of zoos in the United States and the United Kingdom have discontinued their elephant programs because they simply cannot adequately provide for the needs of these animals. There are many unusual animals that can be brought into the home, but consider carefully whether this is fair or just to the animal, and whether you can actually provide health care and other resources for her. An exotic hedgehog might be cute, but your local veterinarian will probably have no idea how to care for her when she's ill.

How Much is That Doggie in the Window?

Where to find your companion animal is as important an ethical issue as what kind of animal you can care for. Far too often animals, particularly those in some pet stores, are bred only for money, and as kittens and puppies they're not given the proper veterinary care and socialization they need to be well-adjusted, healthy adult animals. These places, commonly called puppy- or kitten-mills, operate a for-profit businesses and provide as little care as possible in order to keep their costs down. As a general rule of thumb, if someone is willing to sell you an animal without asking you any questions about your environment and ability to care for an animal, you should probably be wary about the care the animal has received so far. Though it can be emotionally difficult not to buy that puppy or kitten who needs a home, resist supporting places that mass produce or sell animals in this way; it only encourages mistreatment of more animals.

You may want to decide if it seems ethical to even shop in a store that sells animals from the puppy and kitten mills. It is one thing to be hospitable and compassionate, but as Christians we also balance our care for others with a sense of informed compassion. Jesus overturned the tables of those who desecrated the temple with their commerce. Choosing to boycott those who abuse animals, or financially support those who do so, is one way of imitating Jesus.

People who genuinely care about the welfare of animals are rightly careful about placing them into homes where the animals will receive the care and affection they need, even at the risk of offending those who want to adopt a pet. Some rescue organizations even focus their efforts on specific breeds if you've got your heart set on a particular one. So many animals (cats, dogs, and other small animals) are left at local shelters or rescue organizations, and need good homes; it's worth considering if you have the love and space to offer to one of these animals.

You may have your heart set on a purebred and documented cat or dog, in which case you may need to look for a breeder. Just like other places to find animals, there are good breeders and bad ones. A good breeder is going to ask you a lot of questions about yourself and your environment, and will want to meet you and others who live in your household to try to match you with the right animal. They'll also be willing to show you the environment in which the animals spend most of their time, and will provide guidance for the care and training of your animal. They will know the animal's health and vaccination history, and will provide a guarantee that the animal is healthy. If a breeder is rushing you through the process, and just seems to want to make a sale, you're wise to be wary.

Love at First (or Second) Sight
I've watched it happen over and over, and it's happened to me as well. People wander down the aisles in an animal shelter, and a particular dog or cat catches their eye. It's love at first sight. There

does seem to be something intuitive that draws many of us to just the right animal. A friend of mine, Susan, whose husband died a few years ago was ready for a new animal companion in her home, and we were both looking at kittens that a friend of ours was fostering for the local shelter. Susan fell for one of the kittens right away, and the kitten seemed to fall for her as well. The little female kitten curled up in her arms, purring madly, as if she were trying to convince Susan to take her home (and it worked!).

Many of us who live with animals have had this experience. When you're trying to select the right animal to bring home, pay attention to those pulls toward one animal or another. But temper them with a rational approach as well. When my family and I went to find a dog to adopt recently, we selected two dogs who looked like they might meet our criteria (medium size dog, a year or two old). We asked to spend some time with the dogs, but one of the staff at the shelter thought a different dog, and not the two we wanted to look at, was going to be right for us. She gave us a little history of the two we'd selected, and we decided she was right about them, and spent some time instead with Paris, a lab/hound mix, who was, in fact, a great fit for us. Talk to the people who know the animals when you're selecting them. Spend some time with the animal as well. Shelters, as well as breeders, will provide a place for you to play with the animal for a while to get more of a sense of her personality and temperament. Sometimes the most assertive animals get our attention first—they have little fear about presenting themselves to us—while their gentler siblings hang out at the back of the cage. You may want an animal that is active, assertive, and energetic. You might also find a quieter animal more suitable for your environment. So spend some time trying to get to know the animal or animals that catch your eye.

As wonderful as it is to simply fall in love with an animal, try not to forget about the criteria you've set for selecting a companion. A friend of mine fell in love with the picture of a dog from a rescue organization. The dog was just what she and her husband were looking for, one who could travel with them, a female, and a dog that didn't shed much. They went to meet her one day, and were very disappointed. The dog didn't really look like she had in the picture, and she smelled terrible (she hadn't had a bath since giving birth two months before.) Even worse, the dog didn't seem to like them. They went home without her. But over the next two weeks, my friend couldn't stop thinking about the dog, and finally decided that there must be some reason that this dog belonged with them. They had a hard time convincing the rescue organization folks that they really planned to give this dog a permanent home, but were finally able to do so, and took the terrier home.

At first the dog was just as terrible as she'd been at the rescue organization. She eliminated all over her crate, barked incessantly, and tried to open the bedroom door with her teeth. The terrier had probably been treated badly in the past, since she was terrified of brooms. But over time, and with some training and much love, the terrier became an affectionate, housetrained, and loyal, and very funny member of the household, a dog that my friends now adore. These same friends adopted another rescue dog less than a year later, one that they fell in love with at first sight. Both dogs are treasured and respected members of the family.

Whether you fall in love at first sight, or whether you listen to an inner voice that tells you that somehow this is the right companion for you, take whatever time you need to find the newest member of the household. Ignatius's spiritual wisdom, referred to in chapter one, is as valuable here as it is in discerning whether or not an animal fits into your home and life. Spend some time imagining how the animal will fit into your household, and if this is an animal God calls you to care for. Ask yourself, too, as Ignatius put it, "to which side reason inclines." A little prayer never hurts either. Consider adding this one to your daily prayers while you're seeking a new companion:

O God, grant us in all our doubts and uncertainties the grace
to ask what you would have us do; that the spirit of wisdom
may save us from all false choices, and that in your light we may
see light, and in your straight path may not stumble,
through Jesus Christ our Lord.
—William Bright

CHAPTER FOUR
Let Me Introduce You

∂∂∂∂

"I was a stranger and you welcomed me. . . ." —Matthew 25:35

On his way home with a brand new beagle puppy, a friend of mine and his family stopped at their church and asked their priest to bless the animal as a new member of their home, which the priest did. I suspect, however, that there are more than a few ministers and priests who would be surprised by such a request, but to me it sounded like a fine way to welcome a new member of the family.

"All guests who present themselves are to be welcomed as Christ," wrote St. Benedict, the sixth-century writer of a *Rule* for monastic living. "Proper honor must be shown to all."[25] Benedict's instructions for guests included that they receive the prayers of the monks, and the kiss of peace (a warm greeting), and then Benedict recommended, as mentioned before, that they be given water for washing, as well as food and a comfortable place to sleep. Benedict also had a special recommendation for guests who were poor or on pilgrimage: "Great care and concern are to be shown in receiving poor people and pilgrims, because in them more particularly Christ is received."[26] It is worth remembering this instruction when a stray animal, and particularly one who looks as if she has been without care for a while, shows up at the door.

The animals we bring to live with us may not be presenting themselves—except, perhaps, for those strays—but Benedict's instruction to welcome the stranger warmly makes as much sense for our animal companions as it does for human guests. The Celts knew this centuries ago when St. Columba called some of the monks together and bade them to go wait on a particular shoreline. "For when the third hour before sunset is past," he told them, "there shall come flying from the northern coast of Ireland a strange guest, a crane, wind tossed and driven far from her course in the high air: tired out and weary will she fall on the beach at thy feet and lie there, her strength nigh gone."[27] Columba advised them to care for the crane—their guest—for three days, after which she would resume her journey. The monks went to the shore where they'd been directed, and cared for the crane who appeared just as Columba has predicted. To welcome any of God's creatures—two-legged or four or more—and to make them feel at home is to welcome and honor God's presence in our homes.

What's Welcoming

Helping a new animal feel welcome in your home is about considering what will feel most like hospitality to him. Bringing a new animal into a home and promptly introducing it to the resident animal(s) is unlikely to feel hospitable to anyone, and it may result in difficult relationships between the animals that can be challenging to repair. A throng of people surrounding the new animal, all trying to talk and play with him at the same time, may not feel very welcoming either. Many animals need some time and space to adjust to a new environment, to check out the new smells and the lay of the land. You and other family members may be very excited about the new addition to the family and want to interact with her immediately, but plan a welcome for your new companion that meets her needs so the adjustment and eventual fit into the family is as easy as possible.

If you're bringing home a species of animal that you've never lived with before, take some time to find out what will make that animal's transition into your home as easy and relaxing as possible. When someone came to St. Benedict's monastery, asking admission, he was allowed to come in and stay in the guest quarters for a while, and only after that would he enter the quarters where the monks lived. Benedict wisely provided a transitional space, allowing the person to be first a guest, and then later, a member of the family. Your new animal will need the same kind of transitional time and space. Cats, in general, benefit from a quiet, closed room with plenty of furniture to hide under for a few hours or even a few days. Rescue animals—animals from a shelter or from a rescue organization—may also find an enclosed and quiet space the most welcoming. Other animals, such as a new puppy, may be fine running around the house interacting with people fairly quickly. A new guinea pig is going to hide under anything it can find for a while. Every animal is different; pay attention to what the specific animal you're bringing home might need.

If you're bringing home an animal to a household where other animals already live, pay particular attention to the introduction of the animals to each other. Often animals will do better with slow introductions over a period of time rather than just tossing them together. The new animal will probably be grateful for his own area, free of other household animals, for a few days or longer. Use a spare bedroom or den or some other space that you can close off, but be sure that you've prepared the space and that it's safe for the animal.

If the new cat or dog has not yet been checked over by your own veterinarian to make sure that she's healthy, be sure to make an appointment for the new animal as soon as possible, and keep the animals separated until after the appointment. Keeping animals isolated from one another for a period of time also gives them a chance to get used to the smell of another animal in the house, and even to the idea of a new housemate. If you're not sure what the best strategies are for introducing animals to one another check with your veterinarian, or do some research online or in the various books on the market and in your local library.

Blessing Your New Companion

There is something within most of us that senses the need for blessing. My friend brought his new puppy to his priest for a blessing. It is no longer unusual for those who are leaving a home or moving into a new one to bless the space they are leaving or entering with a house blessing service. Blessings were used in the Bible in many ways; God blesses all sorts of things in the biblical stories, including people, groups, nations, living creatures, food, the Sabbath, and even work. The Jewish people have long practiced blessing things and people; at the beginning of Shabbat (the Sabbath), for instance, they bless the candles, the wine, the bread, and the children. Christians, though we use blessings less often than our Jewish brothers and sisters, also find blessings to be important. Blessings are a way of grounding a relationship in God—of dedicating our relationship to God's purposes. Blessing our new companions is a way of marking this relationship in God's presence, of committing ourselves to the care, nurture, and love of this animal, as well as commending it to God's care.

The following are some blessings you might use with your new animal companion. If the animal is comfortable with your presence you might hold or sit with the animal and place your hands gently upon him. If not, you and any other members of the household could simply gather to read one of these prayers aloud.

Blessing Prayer for Pets

ಶಿಶಿಶಿ

O Supreme Spirit of Creation,
 from Your sacred breath came forth
 birds and beasts, fish and fowl,
 creatures of such variety and beauty
 that we are continuously amazed
 at Your divine imagination.

These children are Yours
 have been blessed by You, their Creator,
 with simplicity, beauty, and a cosmic purpose.

They have been blessed as well
 by our greatest grandfather, Adam,
 who in Edenland gifted each with its own name.

They have also been blessed with protection
     by our ancient ancestor Noah, patron saint of those
     who seek to preserve all that You have created.

Sheep and goats, donkeys and cows,
     doves and serpents, fish and birds of the air
     were blessed by Jesus, Your Son,
     by His being born in their company
     and by making use of them in His teachings.

May we, in this holy pattern, now bless _____ (name)
     by taking delight in his/her beauty and naturalness.
May we bless this animal
     with a Noah-like protection
     from all that might harm him/her.
May we, like Adam and Eve,
     speak to this creature of Yours
     with kindness and affection,
     reverencing his/her life and purpose
     in our communal creation.

May we never treat _____ (name) as a dumb animal,
     but rather let us seek to learn his/her language
     and to be a student of all the secrets that he/she knows.

May your abundant blessing rest upon this creature
who will be a companion for us in the journey of life.
Amen.[27]

—Edward Hays

God, around this table we are gathered as friends and family to give thanks for many things. Let us in our thoughts today especially remember the pets who are our companions. May they never be hungry while in our care, and may they always know and feel and come to understand that our table is set with them in mind also. For we believe, O God, that you have prepared a place for us, and in imitation of your love, we should prepare a place for those we love. May all at this table—under, around, and near it—be blessed with joy in your creation. How great are your works, O God! How wonderful are your deeds! Amen.[29]

—Rayner W. Hesse, Jr.

We call upon you, most blessed Saint Anthony, patron of domestic animals, to bless our pets this day. Protect them from injury, preserve them from illness, and help us provide all that they need. But more than that, inspire us to love them as they love us—unconditionally, unwaveringly, and always. Amen.[30]

—Anthony F. Chiffolo

CHAPTER FIVE

Tell Me Your Name

∂∂∂∂

Then the LORD God said, "It is not good that the man should be alone; I will make him a helper as his partner." So out of the ground the LORD God formed every animal of the field and every bird of the air, and brought them to the man to see what he would call them; and whatever the man called every living creature, that was its name.

—Genesis 2:18-19

"*P*art of the joy of getting a dog is naming it," write the Monks of New Skete, a monastic community with a ministry in training dogs. "In Eden, Adam was given the responsibility of naming the animals and we have inherited this task. A name not only defines, it expresses the hopes we bring to the relationship."[31] Naming is a responsibility, a sacred task passed down from generation to generation, beginning with the first man all the way down to us.

Naming in the biblical texts was a powerful act; God often used a change in names to mark a new status or relationship. But the names given by humans usually expressed something about the essence of the person being named. Esau's name, for instance, means "hairy," the most noticeable physical characteristic of the firstborn son of Rebekah and Isaac. Naming was an intimate act, one that implied knowledge of the person or place being named. Sometimes the names brought with them an explicit or implied covenant. Abram became Abraham when God covenanted with him and promised to make Abraham's descendents numerous (Genesis 17). Adam, as the Monks of New Skete remind us, named all the animals in Genesis 2. "Adam thereby becomes a participant in their very creation," writes religion professor Karla Bohmback, "since names call forth the true nature or essence of that which is named."[32]

To name something or someone is to identify something particular about her or to express your hopes for her. To name someone or something is to have a hand in its ongoing creation, and an ongoing responsibility, relationship, and covenant with the named.

"I want Adam and Adam's children to protect and care for these animals. Maybe if I let Adam name the animals, he will get to know them better and really take care of them."[33] Those are the words that Rabbi Marc Gellman imagines God thinking as God gives Adam the task of naming the animals in the Garden of Eden. Naming, for Gellman, has to do with knowing the creature well, with caring enough to name her, and with caring enough to nurture what we have named. In his story, "Adam's Animals,"—a midrash, or a story about a story—Gellman imagines Adam being overwhelmed with the task at first, so Adam gives all the animals numbers. It's hard to imagine a more impersonal naming strategy! We give numbers to people when we want to de-humanize them, to make them less individual and important. Prisoners are given numbers instead of names. But fortunately, there are so many animals that Adam loses track of his numbering system.

Next, in Rabbi Gellman's charming story, Adam decides to use the words "Hey You!" each time he wants help from one of the creatures. He tries to erase the distinctions among the animals by giving them all the same name. But that backfires too, since none of the animals know which "hey you" Adam is calling at a given moment. Finally a bear, rather fed up with Adam's silly systems, looks Adam in the eye and asks him: "With all your talking you never once thought to ask us—the animals—what we would like to be named. Why don't you try that?"[34] And that, of course, is the secret. The animals tell Adam their names and the problem is solved.

There is wisdom in this contemporary midrash for those of us trying to name an animal. Many animal names, like so many of the biblical ones, come about as the result of observation after spending time with an animal. Sometimes the name seems to come from the dog or cat or hamster directly, just as in the midrash. Lily, one of the cats who lives with me now, seemed to insist on her own name somehow, in a way I can't fully explain. I'd like to claim that she told me her name, but in some sense that would be an exaggeration. A friend of mine, who was nine at the time, gave her the name Emma, and it seemed like a good choice. I tried to use it, but I became frustrated because the name Lily kept coming out of my mouth instead. I don't know where the name came from. There aren't any Lilys in my family. It isn't a name that has any special meaning to me. But somehow the name Emma just didn't seem to "fit" and "Lily" did.

A friend of mine had a dog who seemed to name herself as well. The dog, fresh from the shelter, looked up with interest when the name "Maggie" was suggested to her, so that's the name she got.

"The Naming of Cats is a difficult matter," wrote the poet T.S. Eliot in a poem that later became part of the famous play *Cats*. "It isn't just one of your holiday games."[35] The reason naming an animal, be it cat, dog, guinea pig, or another creature, is difficult is that naming involves intentionality. Ideally a name comes as a result of spending time with the animal and observing something of its nature, and matching that with a name that speaks either of the animal himself, and of your hopes for your life together. I have some friends who often name their animals after Celtic saints. The names reflect their own interest in these historical and religious figures, as well as how each animal's own characteristics match those of an admired saint.

A few words of caution about names come from the Monks of New Skete. "Remember that 'cute' names may sound quaint on puppies . . . but lose their charm when the dog is older. Joke names or names that emphasize a physical characteristic of the breed or individual dog are a matter of personal taste, but generally we recommend against them. Dogs are remarkably sensitive, and often seem to intuit when they are the butt of sarcasm."[36] Though the monks' advice is about dogs in particular, it holds true for animals in general.

That the act of naming is intentional doesn't mean it has to be solemn or tedious, anymore than choosing the name of a child needs to be. Some years ago, when I decided I needed a cat—my first one as an adult—I went looking for a cat that was willing to be named Codi. I'd been thinking for a while about adding a cat to the household, and I'd finished a novel with a character named Codi, a figure I admired. I wanted a cat who would bring some of the same energy and intelligence of that fictional heroine into my home. And so, I went to the Humane Society to find a cat who was willing to be named Codi. All the cats and kittens in the place backed up in their cages, moving away from me, except one. A beautiful black and white kitten moved forcefully to the front of his cage and pushed his head against the bars, trying to force his head through the bars to connect with my hand. We'd chosen one another. Codi came home with me that day, and turned out to be just as classy as the heroine he was named for.

If naming the animal is a family affair, let everyone have a part in it. Grab a baby name book and look for a name that speaks of whatever you've observed about the creature, as well as your hopes for the relationship with him. Are there any great religious or historical figures, or any other person who is important to you, whose characteristics the animal somehow emulates? Is there, perhaps, some name that just keeps presenting itself to you that seems to be the name of your companion? Just let the ideas fly. A friend of mine had a family contest to name their new dachshund puppy. The seven-year-old piped up first with the name "Longjohn." For him, longjohns were bakery treats, associated with a local bakery he visited regularly with his mother. Longjohns, éclair-like pastries, looked like the dachshund, and they were good. One could do worse than name the dog after something much beloved.

Obviously, this process doesn't always result in a name deeply fraught with historical or religious meaning or importance. It is the practice of intentionality—of choosing a name carefully—that matters here. My step-son named his female kitten "Stripe." The name made little sense to me or to his dad. After all, the kitten is almost solid gray with hardly a stripe on her, and somehow the name "Stripe" didn't seem like a name for a female. But the name made sense to Christian, and this was to be his kitten, so "Stripe" it was. And though Stripe hasn't developed many stripes, still she knows her name, and it seems to be one that expresses the relationship between Christian and the cat. In fact, it's hard to imagine her with any other name now.

Sometimes animal companions, particularly adult ones, come with a name in place, and it may be difficult for the animal if you change the name. Friends of mine adopted two cats from a friend of theirs who was moving and couldn't take the cats with them. The cats had Hebrew names, which my friends kept out of respect for both the cats, and also their Jewish friend. If your companion knows his name and responds to it, it may be best to leave the name alone, but there's also biblical precedent for changing the animal's name to reflect her new situation. In biblical times, if your circumstances changed, sometimes your name changed too, as it did for Abraham. Monks and nuns today, when joining a religious order, take a new name to signify their new relationship with Christ. As with all things related to our animal companions, take the animal's comfort into account when making a decision to change his name. If she is an older animal and quite accustomed to responding to a particular name, you may cause more discomfort by changing it than by living with the name the animal came with.

Since naming is a covenant between you and the animal, the brief liturgy that follows can be used to acknowledge the power and privilege of naming, and the responsibilities that go along with it. You can use this liturgy even if you're keeping the name an animal came with. If this is to be done as a family or community, gather everyone together in a circle, and designate someone to hold the animal, or put the animal's cage in the center of the circle. Create a space that feels comfortable and safe for the humans and especially for the animal. Designate someone to ask the covenanting questions, and encourage all those who will be caring for the animal to take the vows. This service is simple enough even for young children to use with your help; older children can even read the part of "One" below. If you live alone, or are the sole provider for the animal, simply adjust the service above for private use. Sit with your animal and speak the vows to the animal. (For instance, "I name you _____. I promise to care for you as God's own creature," and so on.)

Covenanting with Animals: A Liturgy

One:	Will you name this creature?
Respondent:	(The name of the animal is given)
One:	Will you care for (Name) as God's own creature?
Respondent:	I will with God's grace.
One:	Will you be mindful of (Name's) Christ-like vulnerability?
Respondent:	I will be so mindful.
One:	Will you love and protect (Name) so long as he/she lives?
Respondent:	I will with God's grace.
One:	Will you be faithful and kind in good times and bad?
Respondent:	I promise to be so faithful.

Participants may touch/pat/stroke the animal as a sign of the covenant affirmed between them.

One: May the God of the new covenant of Jesus
            Christ grant you grace to fulfill your promise
            and to show mercy to other creatures as God
            has shown mercy to you. Amen.[37]

Congregations in a variety of denominations these days offer
opportunities to bless animals, and these services are a good time to
remember this covenant you're making. For some suggestions about
liturgies for blessing the animals see the appendix.

PART TWO

The Covenant in Daily Life

∂∂∂∂

It is not in romance but in routine that the possibilities for

transformation are made manifest. And that requires

commitment. [38]

—*Kathleen Norris*

*F*inding a companion animal, preparing for its presence in the household, and bringing the animal home are always new and exciting, even if you've done this many times before. Each animal is new to you. Each animal has her own personality, gifts, and challenges to discover. But it is in the ordinary—and occasionally extraordinary—days that follow that the real relationship develops. You've made a sacred covenant with your new companion, and that covenant gets lived not just once or twice, but in day-to-day life. Think of it in terms of any relationship; it isn't until the infatuation wears off a bit that we really get to know someone. The same is true with our animal companions. Walking the dog, even when the temperature is ten degrees above zero, staying up all night with a sick bird or hamster, changing the cat's litter box—these are the things that test and prove our love. The ordinary and occasionally extraordinary events of daily life are the places where you discover what the covenant and commitments you've made to your companion really mean. In the midst of routine and sometimes dreary work, we learn, or remember, what it means to be God's very ordinary hands and feet in the world.

For the animals we invite into our homes, that's just what we are: God's hands and feet. We are the ones who need to provide the food, shelter, health care, and love that God desires for all of creation. God cares about such simple daily things, like giving the Israelites bread and water throughout their forty-year wandering in the desert between life as slaves in Egypt and the new life in Canaan. In the New Testament, Jesus also focused on the daily and mundane needs of those around him. The five thousand gathered to listen to him needed food at the end of the day, and Jesus helped them figure out how to feed themselves, rather than sending the people away to fend for themselves as the disciples had suggested. Jesus often shared meals with his friends and disciples, and even with tax-collectors. Jesus also washed the ordinary feet of his disciples, and, although the miracle was extraordinary, the water that became wine was very ordinary.

God cares about the physical needs of all that exists, but without our hands and feet God's hopes and dreams cannot come to full fruition. We are God's hands when we feed the bird or groom the cat (activities that shouldn't be done at the same time!). We are God's feet when we take the dog out for a walk, or when we put the gerbil in his bubble to roll around the house for a while.

This, more than anything else, serves to remind us that spiritual practices are not just about meditation and other activities that draw us inward. Spiritual practices, in the long run, are meant to direct us back outward into the world. "We do not find God solely in the interior realm," write the Monks of New Skete, "and when we live our lives as if we did, we fall victim to a dualism that has profound spiritual consequences. Because we are responsible for living creatures, needy and vulnerable, our dogs help ground us in reality, forcing us to appreciate the mystery of God in all its length and breadth."[39]

To care for an animal and do it well, from a place of compassion and concern for all of creation, is a spiritual practice because it connects us with the source of everything, which is God. Feeding, playing, and training are all ways of deepening a relationship with God's creatures. Caring for an animal when she is sick, changing the litter box or bedding materials, and grooming are ways of sharing Christ's compassion.

These regular tasks can also become prayers if we choose. Feeding an animal, for instance, becomes an opportunity for thanksgiving for the food we have and can provide, and a time to pray for all creatures who don't have adequate food. Playing with your companion can remind you of the joy of God's good earth, and might encourage us to pray for those who find little joy in their lives right now. If you're willing, the relationship you have with your animal companion can open you up to a deeper understanding of the interconnectedness of everything that exists, and then to prayer. "God . . . holds everything in being," Ignatian spirituality author Margaret Silf writes, "continually impelling all creation in the direction of Life. Prayer is our response to this reality, the expression of our deep desire to be in right relationship with its Source and Sustainer. This in turn can lead us into right relationship with each other and the world."[40]

Tending to the daily or regular needs of our companions is also a way of being of service to God's creation, as we were asked to do in Genesis. It is easy to get caught up in our own needs, and sometimes that's necessary, but it is through service to the world around us that we imitate Jesus best. As St. Benedict reminds us: "The second step of humility is that a man loves not his own will nor takes pleasure in the satisfaction of his desires; rather he shall imitate by his actions that saying of the Lord: 'I have come not to do my own will, but the will of him who sent me' (John 6:38)."[41] Taking care of the routine and daily tasks involved in caring for companion animals are ways of following Jesus, of being one who serves.

Acting in the role of God's hands and feet and heart, of course, requires that we attend to our own spiritual lives. The well from which energy and love are drawn in meeting the obligations we've taken on is God, and without attention to our own spiritual life— through prayer, meditation, worship, Sabbath times, play, and care of our own bodies—we'll quickly run out of resources from which to pull strength. As you read through the chapters in this section, think about the ways in which the food you eat, the ways in which you play and rest, and the care you give to your own body are important spiritual practices that can sustain you as you provide these services to others.

The chapters that follow in part two are about the simple and often daily things we do as part of the covenant we've made with our companions. Feeding, cleaning, training, and playing are the arenas in which we deepen our relationship with our animals and with God.

> God of Love, help us to remember
> that Christ has no body now on earth but ours,
> no hands but ours, no feet but ours.
> Ours are the eyes to see the needs of the world.
> Ours are the hands with which to bless everyone now.
> Ours are the feet with which he is to go about doing good.
> —St. Teresa of Avila

O merciful Creator, your hand is open wide to satisfy the needs of every living creature: Make us always thankful for your loving providence; and grant that we, remembering the account that we must one day give, may be faithful stewards of your good gifts; through Jesus Christ our Lord, who with you and the Holy Spirit lives and reigns, one God, for ever and ever. Amen.[42]

> —*The Book of Common Prayer*

CHAPTER SIX

When I Was Hungry You Fed Me

࿔࿔࿔࿔

O Lord, how manifold are your works!
in wisdom you have made them all;
the earth is full of your creatures.

All of them look to you
to give them their food in due season.

You give it to them; they gather it;
you open your hand, and they are filled with good things.
    —Psalm 104: 24, 27-28 (BCP)

"*I*t was the custom of the most blessed high-priest Moling to feed animals, both wild and domestic, in honor of their Creator," the story of "Saint Moling's Fox and the Hens" begins, "and they used to take food from his hand."[43] There are many stories from the Desert Fathers and from the Celtic and other saints about feeding the animals; perhaps the saintly people in our history found this to be a special joy.

Some of the stories simply document people feeding hungry animals. A desert hermit plucks figs from a tree to feed a lion, who eats them right from the man's hand. The Celtic St. Cuthbert, though fasting for spiritual reasons on his journey, makes sure his horse has enough to eat. A wolf waits outside the hut of an unnamed desert dweller each day, and he gives her whatever bread is left over from his very frugal meal.

Other stories revolve around animals eating the right things. A fox, upon stealing one of the monk's books to eat, is scolded by St. Moling; the fox brings the book back, and never tries to eat another one. St. Macarius of Alexandria heals the whelp of a hyena who tries to thank him by killing a sheep and bringing him the sheepskin. Macarius makes her promise never to steal and kill another sheep, but to come to him in the future if she is hungry and he will feed her. In some of the stories the animals even find food for people who are hungry. Caring for one another by providing food is a sacred duty, done, as the story of St. Moling says, to honor the Creator of us all.

But there's more to the task of feeding your companion than just providing food, as the stories occasionally illustrate. Part of our covenant with the animals is to provide healthy food in the right proportions for the animal at a particular stage of its life. In one of the stories told about the Celtic St. Brendan, he and those traveling with him come upon an old man on an island. The old man, barely more than skin and bones, warns them to flee the island quickly as there is a cat there who has grown huge—perhaps as big as a small ox—from eating so many fish over the years. The cat in this story had helped himself to the fish available on a small pool on the island, a pool that was restocked daily by the tides, and had grown, over the years, into something mean and out-of-control. The cat, apparently, could swim as well, and came charging after Brendan and his crew fleeing the island, threatening their lives until another beast from the sea swallowed the cat.[44] We do a great disservice to the animals we live with when we over-feed them or feed them foods that aren't healthy for them. A fat cat might be cute, but it won't be healthy, and its life will be shorter and much less comfortable than it could be otherwise.

What and how we feed our companions might not seem like ethical questions, but they are; they are part of the covenant we've made with the animals we live with. In the larger sense feeding the animals is a way of responding to God's trust in our abilities to care for the creation. In Genesis 1:28, God gives people dominion over all the animals on earth. "Be fruitful and multiply," God tells Adam and Eve, "and fill the earth and subdue it; and have dominion over the fish of the sea and over the birds of the air and over every living thing that moves upon the earth." The dominion God grants Adam and Eve—and us, by extension—is often misunderstood and misused. Writing about the use of the word *dominance* in Genesis, biblical scholar Walter Brueggemann explains: "The dominance is that of a shepherd who cares for, tends, and feeds the animals. . . . [T]he task of 'dominion' does not have to do with exploitation and abuse. It has to do with securing the well-being of every other creature and bringing the promise of each to full fruition."[45]

Part of the care of the animals who live with us, then, is tending to their nutritional needs so that each can become all that God hopes they will be. Each individual animal will need different amounts and kinds of foods at various stages of their lives. Young animals, for instance, need a lot of food and food that supports growth, while older ones will probably need a lower calorie diet, or perhaps even a diet geared toward preventing common health problems. A sick animal may need a very particular diet for a period of time, or perhaps for the rest of her life. Ethical feeding of animals even means curbing some of our own bad habits, such as feeding animals from table scraps or at other times besides feeding times; oftentimes what we are eating at the dinner table or snacking from the refrigerator, mid-afternoon is inappropriate for a healthy animal's diet (not to mention our own!). Part of our covenant with these companions is to learn about our particular animal's nutritional needs so that he can reach his own full potential, and live as long and healthy a life as possible. If you're in doubt about the best diet for your animal at a particular stage of his life, consult with your animal's veterinarian for advice.

The physical act of feeding our companions is also important as it reminds us of our own right relationship with God's creation. We are God's servants and caretakers; we are not the Creator. St. Benedict required all the monks of his monastery to take their turn in serving the others their meals. No one was excused from this duty unless he was sick or away from the monastery on important business. If someone was not very strong, he was given help, but he still took his turn serving, for, as Benedict wrote, that service fostered love within the community. Our service to our companions, in the form of preparing and serving their meals, fosters love and relationship in the same way.

Feeding our animals is sacred work, just like feeding the members of our families. Just as we thank God for the food on our own tables, it is good and right to acknowledge that God uses our hands and feet to provide food for the beloved animals who live in our homes. Consider posting a copy of the psalm found at the beginning of this chapter near your animal's food supply as a reminder of the importance of what you're doing when you feed your companion. Or use any grace you like, or the very simple and traditional prayer below as you prepare your companion's food each day, as a reminder that God feeds each and every one of us. This prayer is simple enough for children to learn if they're helping to feed the animals.

God is great, and God is good,
And we thank Him for our food,
By His hand we all are fed;
Thank you, Lord, for our daily bread.

CHAPTER SEVEN
Training and Compassion

∂∂∂∂

May my teaching drop like the rain, my speech condense like the dew; like gentle rain on grass, like showers on new growth.

—Deuteronomy 32:2

"Often we blame our dogs for being disobedient," the Monks of New Skete write about the dogs they train, "when the real problem lies with us. Being a good trainer and a good companion requires humility, the humility to realize that our own handling abilities with the dogs are continually developing; it's always preferable to presume that the problem lies with us."[46] I first read this sentence not long after being dragged down the street by the sixty-five-pound lab/hound dog we'd adopted from our local shelter. I was pretty sure that the problem lay with the dog, who was around two years old, and the evidence was that he hadn't had a day of obedience training yet in his short life. Nonetheless, the dog wasn't going to train himself, and if walks were going to become fun for both of us, I was the one who was going to have to make that happen.

"Obedience training," words that can send shivers up the spine, strikes some people as both an odious task and a harsh one designed to break an animal's spirit. And there are some training methods for domestic animals that are harsh and do break an animal. Done well and properly, however, training is neither of those things, any more than teaching a child how to behave around others should be harsh or spirit-breaking. Training, done well, as the Monks remind us, has as much or more to do with us as trainers and our ability to approach training with humility, as it does with the animal. Teaching an animal basic obedience should be a mutual process; training is about paying attention to what the animal needs and wants as much as it is about helping her learn particular behaviors. It is about recognizing the behaviors that are natural to the animal— going to the bathroom, for instance—and directing those behaviors in appropriate ways. But more than anything else, training is fundamentally about recognizing that you are working with a creature who, like you, is beloved of God, and according her the same level of respect that God has for her.

Training involves building a relationship with your companion, one that allows both your relationship, and your animal's potential, to blossom.[47] Think about it in human terms for a moment. The process of teaching children, while frustrating at times, is also a time of bonding between a parent, teacher, or friend, and a child. A friend of mine has a young child who gets terribly distressed when things go wrong, and the child often imagines the worst possible scenarios when he can't understand or accomplish something immediately. More often than not, these situations cause the child to erupt in some combination of fury, anxiety, fear, and frustration. My friend, his dad, always responds very gently to these eruptions, becoming quieter as the child becomes more distressed. He always looks for any genuine need that presents itself and responds to it, and provides whatever guidance or solution is truly needed, but he doesn't respond to the anxiety itself. His gentleness and quietness in the face of what looks unmanageable to his son speaks volumes to the boy, who has learned, over the years, that most situations are not as bleak as they appear to be at first. My friend's willingness to listen and to provide an example to his son is allowing his son to put aside his anxieties and reach for his own full potential.

The same is true with our companion animals. Screaming at, hitting, or directing other violent behaviors at an animal who is engaged in disruptive behavior rarely solves anything in the long run, and often it creates a fearful animal. Most trainers say that if you don't catch an animal in the act, any sort of punishment is useless anyway. If you didn't see the dog eliminating on the floor, and you find it an hour later, the dog has long forgotten what he did, and won't equate punishment with the activity. A calm response to problem behaviors, and better yet, calm training before behaviors get out of hand, gives the animal an opportunity to learn in a comfortable environment, so he can be the best companion possible.

St. Francis gives us some sense of what a calm approach to a problem animal might look like. A wolf was terrorizing the town of Gubbio once; any person or animal who strayed outside the town was devoured by the wolf. St. Francis, who had compassion for the people—but also for the wolf—went out into the countryside to talk to the wolf. As he approached, the wolf prepared to attack Francis, but the saint moved toward the wolf calmly, saying, "Come here, Brother Wolf! In the name of Christ I command you to do no harm either to me or to anyone else."[48] The wolf stopped in his tracks, and St. Francis made a deal with him. If the wolf would stop attacking the people and animal of the village, the people would provide for him a regular supply of food. The wolf then accompanied Francis back to the village, where the amazed people agreed to their side of the bargain. The townspeople and the wolf co-existed peacefully from that time forward.

Francis's calm response, of course, is easier said than done when your companion has made you crazy for the fifth time today, but it is possible. When we first brought our dog, Paris, home from the shelter, he liked to jump on us. When I'd walk in the door, sixty-five pounds of dog would come flying at me, and the result usually involved me and a renewed acquaintance with the hardwood floor. Getting mad at Paris for jumping wasn't going to change his behavior in any way, so what we finally learned to do—thanks to a great dog trainer in our area—was to tether him to a lead that is screwed into the baseboard of the wall. Each time he jumps, he gets tethered there for a few minutes until he calms down. The tethering isn't painful to Paris; he's in the room with everyone else, and not isolated. But a few minutes on the lead gives him (and us!) time to calm down and let go of our own anger, and when he's done "serving his time" we can proceed with training or whatever we're doing together. Best of all, Paris stopped jumping on us within a few days.

Obedience

The word "obedience" comes from a Latin root that means "to listen." This means that there is mutuality in training, the kind of mutuality my friend exhibits with his son. The story is told of St. Godric, a saint from the twelfth century, and his cow who needed to be put out to pasture each day and brought in, as well as milked. The young boy who was supposed to care for the cow often forgot his task, so Godric went to the cow one day, showed her the way to the fields, and spoke to her. "I command you in the name of the Lord that every day at sunrise, without anyone leading you, you go forth on your own to your pasture; and every noon and evening, when the proper time comes, you come home without any servant to guide you. And when your udders are full of milk and need milking, come to me wherever I am."[49] The cow did as she was commanded, going to the fields at the appointed times, returning home on her own, and whenever she needed milking she went and found the saint, who milked her. The point of this charming tale is simple: There is obedience—listening—on both sides here. Godric provided for the cow's nutritional needs, but he didn't just send the cow out into the field on a strict and unbreakable schedule; he let her know that whenever she needed him he was available.

The process of training an animal, far from breaking her spirit, should be more about helping the animal to understand what is expected from her and what kinds of interactions are acceptable, as well as teaching her behaviors that will keep her safe. Many animals find the establishment of a routine comforting and helpful, much as young children do. This is particularly true of animals that have been rescued from a shelter, which is usually a chaotic, noisy, and stressful environment. Consistent behaviors on our part help an animal feel a sense of confidence and comfort so she can develop to the fullest. Over the years I've adopted two cats from rescue shelters who were terrified of everything and everyone. Each was afraid to be approached, touched, or held. They would either run away when someone came near them, or duck as if they were afraid of being hit. By being very patient, spending time in the room with them, and letting them approach me in their own time, I found that both cats eventually relaxed and became loving cats. One even developed into a lap cat, jumping on me the instant I sat down anywhere.

Obedience and training are about listening and attending to the animal's needs, as well as about the respectful and affectionate bonds that are formed in the process. Training is not about establishing power over an animal, and it should never involve cruelty or anger. It is about working with an animal, knowing what his body language means, and establishing boundaries of good and poor behavior. Training is about developing a deeper relationship with your companion, one that nurtures a willingness and desire to live together in harmony on both your part and the animal's.

Training is as much about you as the trainer as it is about your companion. In order to be good listeners, to be able to give respect and receive it in return in training, in order to nurture the relationship, our own souls must be in good working order. We need to be able to put aside our own needs, as Jesus often did, to pay attention to the needs of others—our animals—as we work with them. In the New Testament Jesus often goes somewhere apart from the crowds to pray in silence. We have to assume this was a time of focusing, or listening for God's guidance for his own life. And yet, when he was needed, when his disciples sought him out, Jesus was ready to listen to them and respond to whatever need they presented.

We need that same combination of attention to our own spiritual lives and a willingness to be present to others if we're to be good trainers. "Meditation," as the Monks of New Skete write, "is valuable in any human life, because it teaches us how to be calm and fully conscious of what we are thinking and feeling. This experience and personal knowledge enables us to be more appropriate and effective in our communication and behavior."[50]

Having your own spiritual house in order is one of the best tools in training, no matter what method you use. Those of you who are parents know this is true with your children as well. I like the suggestion of the Monks of New Skete, who suggest a short period of meditation before a training session.

First sit down and be quiet for a few seconds. Focus and center yourself by taking a few deep breaths. Let go of any tensions and anxieties you may be harboring and move your attention onto your dog. Become aware of the actual concerns you have for your dog and let that be the foundation from which your training proceeds. When you feel clear, calm, and relaxed, try to visualize the session you intend to have. Recall what you had difficulty with in the previous session and then go through the exercises one by one in your imagination, trying to anticipate possible scenarios that may take place, as well as the response you would hope to provide in each variation.[51]

This exercise helps you to get your own focus off whatever concerns you're carrying around at the time, and focus, instead, on what your companion will need from you in the training session. If you have difficulty putting the day's concerns aside, try to picture them on a table in front of you, and move them to one side for now. Let them know that they're important, and that you'll come back to them in a little while. If you find that you can't put your concerns aside for now, then consider postponing the training session.

Training, of course, is more of an issue with some animals than others. Animals who roam freely around the house, or who have behaviors than can be disruptive in the household, need training, whereas training isn't really an issue with an aquarium of fish. Some animals, such as dogs, benefit from training sessions to help the dog and trainer learn basic obedience commands. Other animals, such as cats, don't really respond to training sessions, but benefit from a clear set of expectations and boundaries applied fairly and consistently. And just as an aside, if you think cats can't be trained, think again! I had a cat who jumped on my desk, turned on my computer printer, and jammed the paper every time she wanted attention, which was usually about five times a day. She knew the sound of it would bring me running. The first time I choose not to come, she peered around the top of the stairs and looked at me with a quizzical look. But she stopped jumping on my printer when I stopped responding. Responding to bad behaviors, even when your response is to yell or punish—in essence rewarding bad behaviors with attention—is just as much training in the animal's eyes as is a more focused effort on rewarding good behavior.

For the animals that do require training there are many different methods, depending on the animal. Your local pet store or public library will probably have a variety of books that describe possible training methods. In most cities there are also places where you can get help or take an obedience class with your animal. If you're not sure what might be most helpful with your companion, consult your veterinarian; he or she is probably familiar with methods and local trainers or schools that can help. Any animal that is roaming freely around the house or outside, or that is in contact with others, needs some training. Failing to train an animal who has free reign of the space is a failure to keep our covenant with our companions. Just as we teach a child not to touch a hot stove, we need to help our animals learn behaviors that will protect them and keep them healthy and happy.

That brings us back to the understanding that effective training has a lot to do with the trainer. Few training manuals address this aspect of training, but we are poor trainers when we are exasperated with our companions, or when we are trying to bring about correct behaviors by sheer force. Whether you are conducting a training session, or simply trying to introduce or correct behaviors throughout the day, knowing your own state of mind and soul makes a difference. If you're angry with a colleague at work and take that out on the cat, she's not going to understand what's wrong, any more than a young child would understand that kind of anger. If training isn't going well, or if your companion is behaving in ways that you just can't cope with right now, give the animal or yourself a "time out"; take some time away from each other and wait for things to cool down a little bit.

I had a kitten once who knew how to push every one of my buttons, and I'd get so irritated with her I sometimes put her in another room for half an hour so I wouldn't explode on her. We're human, and we're going to get angry and frustrated with the animals we live with sometimes, but lashing out at them won't accomplish anything positive. Make sure that you work with or train your companion only when you are calm and clear-headed yourself.

Most of all, remember that your companion is a gift in your life, that she is a beloved creature of God, and is worthy of respect and compassion. Use the following prayer before a training session, or incorporate it into the day in whatever fashion makes sense.

O God, Creator of all things bright and beautiful, we ask your blessing this day on all that is before you, all that is before us, as we gaze upon a world created so that we might live, and move, and have our being. Bless all living things around us, especially the animals that you have given into our care, that our interaction may be one of peace and harmony in living; help us to learn from them, and they from us, about your purpose for this world; and may we remember that we are created from the same primal dust, to which we all return. In a life replete with challenges, a life of joy and sadness, or great gatherings and lonely places, surround us with the Spirit of mutual respect, one for the other, and make us companions along the way.[52]

—Rayner W. Hesse, Jr.

CHAPTER EIGHT
The Covenant and the Litter Box

❧❧❧❧

"Whatever your task, put yourself into it, as done for the Lord. . . .
—Colossians 3:23

Not too long ago the cat of some friends of mine was run over by a car. Their children, ages seven and twelve, mourned the loss of the cat for a few days, but then started lobbying their parents to get some fish to replace their cat. Their mother thought about that for a few days, as the lobbying continued and intensified, and finally she said to her children: "If you want a fish apiece, you have to be willing to take responsibility for the fish. I have four other animals to care for. If you don't feed the fish or clean their bowl, they will die. Are you willing to take on that responsibility?" Her children thought about it for awhile, and came back saying no. I wonder what would have happened if Mom had listed feeding as a responsibility, but not cleaning the bowl. Would the answer have been different? Feeding animals doesn't usually seem too onerous, but cleaning up after them . . . well, that's a different matter. Our new dog, either excited or anxious or both, had an "accident" in his crate at 2 AM on the second night he was with us, and being dragged from sleep by a barking dog, letting him outside, and putting his soiled bed coverings in the washing machine was not terribly exciting. There's little glamour in cleaning out the guinea pig habitat, the fish bowl, or the litter box, or walking the dog with plastic bag in hand.

And yet, it is in these daily, unrelenting tasks—ones that once done will be done again later that day, tomorrow, or a few days from now—that our covenant is kept, our respect shown, and our hospitality extended to the companions God has given us to care for. These small daily tasks are significant, as the poet and author Kathleen Norris writes: "The comfortable lies we tell ourselves regarding these 'little things'—that they don't matter, and that daily personal and household chores are of no significance to us spiritually—are exposed as falsehoods when we consider that reluctance to care for the body is one of the first symptoms of extreme melancholia. Shampooing the hair, washing the body, brushing the teeth, drinking enough water, taking a daily vitamin, going for a walk, as simple as they seem, are acts of self-respect."[53] Just as the failure to care for ourselves signals a difficulty with self-image, the failure to take care of these daily things for our companion animals indicates a lack of respect for them. I was at the Shelter recently and was told of a dog who had been rescued from what the staff there called an "animal hoarder." The woman from whose home the dog was removed had kept nineteen dogs there, none of them properly cared for. The adult dogs weren't even house-broken, and the animals lived in filth. It is difficult to imagine too many environments more disrespectful to domestic companions. Bathing our animals, de-fleaing them, trimming their toenails, and cleaning up their habitats show respect for the creatures God created and entrusted to us.

In biblical days washing the feet of guests was an act of hospitality that any host was expected to perform. As Jesus ate with a Pharisee one night a woman from the city came in to him and began to wash his feet, first with her tears, and then with ointment (Luke 7:36–50). When the Pharisee objected that Jesus was allowing a sinner to touch him, Jesus responded to him: "I entered your house; you gave me no water for my feet, but she has bathed my feet with her tears and dried them with her hair." The host was remiss in his duty here, a duty that the woman from the city fulfilled instead. Later, at the Last Supper, Jesus washed the feet of his own disciples, much to their discomfort. But as Jesus completed his task, he instructed the disciples to follow his example (John 13:14).

We continue to be uncomfortable with the idea of washing another's feet, or even having our own feet washed. It seems . . . well, so servile. Which is the point. Jesus served his own disciples, and we are asked to follow that example, and serve others. We serve our animals when we make sure that they have healthy and clean environments, that they are themselves kept clean and free of pests, and that their bodily needs are met.

In caring for the bodily needs of an animal, and caring for his environment, we are once again acting as God's hands and feet in the world, working to bring God's dream for all of creation into being. In order to do that, we have to learn what kinds of care our companion needs. How often does his environment need to be cleaned, and what are ways of cleaning it that are safe for the animal? Does your companion need to be bathed or groomed regularly, and how can you do that in a way that is safe and comfortable for him? What products will be safe and helpful in keeping the animal free of harmful pests? And how do you clip the toenails of a dog or cat anyway? (If you're really brave you could learn to brush the teeth of your dog or cat; I tried it once with a cat, but that was plenty for me.) Learn about your companion's needs in these areas, either from books, a trainer, or a friend who has experience with your species of animal, or from your veterinarian. And consider approaching these tasks not as items on your to-do list, but as sacred responsibilities, and as service to God's good creation.

Catholic priest Edward Hays provides a wonderful prayer for cleaning the house in his book *Prayers for a Planetary Pilgrim*. That prayer, which focuses on our role as God's co-creators, and on our service to creation, is equally appropriate to cleaning your animal's environment, or the animal herself. You might use this prayer before you clean your animal's habitat, or wash or groom your companion.

✍✍✍✍

May this work that I will begin
be a prayerful re-creation of my world;
may I bring order out of chaos
as my Beloved Creator brought order
on the first day of creation.[54]
—Edward Hays

CHAPTER NINE

Play Time

∽ටටටට

Make a joyful noise to the LORD, all the earth. —Psalm 98:4

Nights at our house sound like the "Indy 500." Thomas and Stripe, two of the younger cats, can be heard chasing each other up and down the stairs, stopping occasionally to wrestle for a few moments before taking out after one another again. During the day I frequently see one of these two lying in wait for the other one, pouncing the minute the unsuspecting partner turns the corner. They're a constant source of amusement, and a reminder to me not to take life quite so seriously.

The antics of the animals are often funny and entertaining; they are also a reminder that play is an essential part of the covenant we've made with our animals. We are all beings with bodies, bodies that God created and called good, and these bodies need care. Play is one way of caring for the physical needs of our companions. Walks or playtimes (with humans or other appropriate animals) are a source of much-needed exercise for our animals, especially when the house, or an animal's habitat, doesn't provide the space for energetic movement. We schedule our children for soccer, softball, and other sports, and help them find enjoyable ways to exercise so they don't become overweight or sluggish; our animals need this same kind of attention. But play is also a way of meeting some of their emotional and relational needs. More often that not play turns into an experience of bonding between an animal and someone he trusts enough to play with.

The play of young animals, in particular, is also educational; animals discover their abilities and their limits through much of their playtime. Playing with your animal may also help you correct behavioral problems, and help prevent stress, loneliness, or depression (that result in behavioral problems) in your companion; and it will keep your animal younger longer. All of that sounds a bit heavy duty, as if play's primary purpose is to cross something off your to-do list. Play often does lead to positive results, like those listed above, and we owe our animals play dates and playtimes as much as we owe them to our children. But play is also an opportunity for us and our animals to be joyful and playful and have fun, to revel in the bodies that we and our companions have been given. Besides, I suspect God enjoys hearing laughter afoot in the world. When Sarah heard that she was to become pregnant at an advanced age, she laughed, and that didn't deter God from fulfilling the promise of a child. When God restored the fortunes of Zion, the Psalmist writes:

"Then our mouth was filled with laughter, and our tongue with shouts of joy" (Psalm 126:2). The animals we live with know instinctively how good playing feels; most of us who are adults need to be reminded from time to time. Spending time with your companion is a good way to re-learn the value of play.

If you have more than one animal in the house the animals can sometimes entertain themselves and play together, as our cats do. But having multiple animals in the house doesn't absolve you from the covenant you made with each of them. When we brought Paris (our dog) home from the shelter, which was a source of stress for the cats (to put it mildly!), we gave the cats a dog-free room where they could feel safe as they got used to the new arrangement. No sooner did we do that than our carpenter decided it was the time to work on the bathroom renovation we'd been planning for six months. The bathroom is right next to the cats' room, so all of a sudden their quiet and safe space, away from the dog, was filled with the noise of drills, hammers, and other unpleasant sounds. The cats took off for the basement for the day, away from the dog and the carpenter. There wasn't a whole lot I could do to make their day more pleasant, but later after the carpenter was gone and the dog was in his crate for the night, I spent a half hour in the cats' room encouraging them to play with me using their favorite toy. It took a while for everyone to relax enough to play. Lily, our most easily frightened cat, didn't come out from under the armchair for at least twenty minutes. But eventually everyone came out and played with me, and then settled down for the night, a lot more relaxed than they had been during the day.

Playing with your companions is a way of bonding with them, even if there are multiple animals in the household. Besides, it's just plain fun most of the time. I'll grant you that walking the dog at ten o'clock at night in snow and ice is less than entertaining, but there's nothing quite like watching the dog run and frolic with other dogs in the dog park on a nice spring day. Or twirling a string for the cat to leap up and catch. I still think with great fondness of that afternoon I spent with the parakeet who liked to walk all around the dining room table shoving all of her toys (which I'd put on the table) off the surface until the table top was completely clean. The abandon with which many animals play—particularly young ones—can be the source of some of the best laughs of the day.

Playtime with your animals doesn't involve spending a fortune on toys, though the selection available at pet stores and through catalogs grows daily. I've found that most animals like the simple stuff and ignore the expensive toys I've gotten for them over the years. Cats enjoy string. Dogs like tennis balls and bones. The bird I bird-sat really enjoyed trying to roll around on a plate with a piece of lettuce and water on it. Gerbils and other small animals usually have fun rolling around the house in a plastic bubble made for that purpose. You can get a lot more complicated and expensive toys, but fancy equipment probably won't make the play session more fun.

I wonder, sometimes, if we buy expensive toys for our companions as a substitute for our own time and attention. With play, as with training, our own spiritual house must be in order; we have to remember how to play, and to be willing to let laughter and playfulness out of their cages inside us. Some years ago a wise spiritual director of mine noticed that I'd put my prayer time on my to-do list, that it had become one more chore to tick off the list each day. Late in the spring that year she asked me to stop praying for the summer, to let play be my prayer for a while. I had absolutely no idea what she was talking about. But I spent the summer going to minor league baseball games on warm summer nights, and hanging out with friends, and playing with my cats, and slowly I began to re-discover a joyful—rather than solely dutiful—connection with my world and with God. At the end of the summer I resumed my prayer practices with a renewed sense of delight, instead of treating them as a task to be accomplished. Our animals know this delight instinctively, or at least they do if it hasn't been taken away from them somehow. In meeting our own covenantal obligations to our companions by playing with them, take some time to notice that the play brings us joy as well; take my spiritual director's advice and let play be your prayer with your animal. If you find that playing with your companion opens you up a little bit to the joy of the world around you, give God thanks for the animal who has been your teacher.

Edward Hays recognizes that joy, playfulness, and humor are gifts of God. His prayer below may help you reflect on playfulness as a sacred activity.

ᴓᴓᴓᴓ

Blessed Are You, Lord our God, Who Invites Us to Be Holy Fools

Father and God of Fools,
Lord of Clowns and Smiling Saints,
we rejoice that You are a God of laughter and tears.
Blessed are You, for You have rooted within us
the gifts of humor, lightheartedness and mirth.
With jokes and comedy, You cause our hearts to sing
as laughter rolls out from us.

We are grateful that Your Son, Jesus, the master of wit,
daily invites us to be fools for Your sake,
to embrace the madness
of Your prophets, holy people and saints.
We delight in that holy madness
which becomes medicine to heal the chaos of the cosmos
since it calls each of us

from the humdrumness of daily life
into joy, adventure
and, most of all, into freedom.

We, who so easily barter our freedom
for illusions of honor and power,
are filled with gratitude that Your Son, by His Life
has reminded us to seek only love,
the communion with each other and with You,
and to balance honor with humor.

With circus bands and organ grinders,
with fools, clowns, court jesters and comedians,
with high spirited angels and saints,
we too join in the fun and foolishness of life,
so that Your holy laughter
may ring out into the edges of the universe.

Blessed are You, Lord our God,
who invites us to be holy fools.

Amen.[55]
—Edward Hays

PART THREE
The Seasons of Life

*W*hen my cat Codi had to be euthanized several years ago due to extreme renal failure, I found that I wasn't really prepared for the moment. Maybe we're never completely ready for these times, but at the time I wished that I'd thought about it—just a bit—ahead of time. Much in the same way that we prepare wills for ourselves, it can be helpful to think ahead and plan for those occasional events in our companion's life that are inevitable. Trying to sort out emotions, the ethical concerns, and the financial questions at times of high stress, when we haven't thought about them at all beforehand, is more painful and challenging than it might be otherwise.

Part Three of this book looks at some of the occasional or one-time events in your companion's life. Decisions about pregnancy are ones to be made very early in the animal's life whenever possible. Other events aren't as predictable. Illness can come upon your companion slowly or suddenly; sometimes you'll have time to think through your response, and at other times you'll find yourself in crisis immediately. Accidents, sometimes minor and other times life-threatening or fatal, often seem to spring out of nowhere. How much medical intervention is enough? When will you turn to palliative care (care that is focused on making your companion comfortable as she proceeds through the process of dying)? Being able to be with a dying animal is a great gift, but thinking ahead about how you'll do that can be helpful. All of us will die someday. What will you do with your companion's remains? How will you acknowledge her death?

You won't be able to map out all of your responses ahead of time; every situation in our lives and in those of our companions present wrinkles and unpredictable emotions that can't be considered ahead of time. While thinking about them ahead of time can't answer all questions, and won't leave you with final answers, it does help. Thinking about these questions in advance is also important when various members of the household might hold differing opinions. Talking about how much medical intervention is enough ahead of time can make that decision just a little easier later on, and allow you to be present to your companion at that difficult time, instead of having to focus attention on the disagreement you and others in your household might be having over the decisions to be made.

CHAPTER TEN

When Two by Two Becomes
Three, Four, or More

❧❧❧❧

And she gave birth to her firstborn son and wrapped him in
bands of cloth, and laid him in a manger.
—Luke 2:7

I vividly remember my first experience of birth with one of
our animals. I was about five years old, and one of our cats
decided to give birth to her kittens on my bed in the middle of the night. I was terrified, and went screaming upstairs to my
parents, fearing what looked like rats all over my bed. At that time
I had no idea that cats usually hide from people when they are giving
birth, and that being present for the birth of the kittens was a great
gift. Many of the events of my early childhood have long ago faded
from memory, but this one remains.

The birth of a new animal is both very ordinary and a great miracle.
Baby animals are born every day all over the world; there is nothing
unusual about pregnancy and birth in general. Yet the ability to give

birth at all, and the bringing forth of a whole new being are both great miracles. That each of us—all living creatures—can begin as small cells that know to form other cells in ways that create a very specific being is truly astonishing. I marvel at this each time a new life appears. And there's hardly anything cuter than a baby animal.

At the same time, our world is overpopulated with animals—baby and otherwise—who need good homes. Every spring and summer shelters are filled with kittens that people hadn't planned for and don't want. Providing a home for an animal and covenanting with that being involves making some decisions about whether or not your companion will be bringing other companions into your life.

Spaying and Neutering

Letting your companion get pregnant is fine if you can care for and want more animals in your home. All life is sacred, and if you have the capacity to care for more animals, keeping the covenant you'll make with them in mind, then you may want to let your animal have a litter. But if you're not planning to care for your animal's babies, and have no definite commitments from anyone else to do so, don't let your animal become pregnant in the first place. Too many of the unwanted baby animals brought forth in our homes end up homeless or euthanized at local shelters. When my family and I adopted our dog at the Shelter recently a woman came in with a box full of kittens, and handed them to the clerk there as if she were handing over a box of bread. I have no idea what her story was; perhaps she'd found these kittens as strays in her garage and was trying to do something good for them. But there are far too many people who—perhaps without thinking about it—let their animals have litters and simply let the babies be a problem for someone else. As people who value all life and count it sacred, each of us needs to do our part to avoid contributing to that problem.

If you have a cat or dog, have her spayed or him neutered even if you only live with the one animal and she or he is primarily an indoor animal. Unless you never open a door or window, your companion may escape someday. And just because you have a male animal doesn't excuse you from worrying about these issues; you're as responsible for your male's behavior as you are for a female and her babies. Sounds like what boys are taught in sex education in school, doesn't it? Even if he or she doesn't ever escape, there are health reasons for spaying or neutering your companion, particularly before they reach sexual maturity. A variety of health problems can be eliminated, or made extremely unlikely through these procedures. The likelihood of some behavioral problems can also be reduced, including spraying, aggression, and especially the misery your female companion feels when in heat. (And if your cat or dog is miserable in heat you can bet that you're going to be miserable too!)

If you're bringing other kinds of animals into your home—guinea pigs, hamsters, birds, rabbits, or others—consider whether you want to adopt just one or multiple animals of the same sex. (Guinea pigs, hamsters, and rabbits can also be neutered.) If you place a male and female of the same species in the same habitat with each other, you should start planning the baby shower early.

It may seem difficult to imagine or worry about pregnancy when you've got a cute little bundle of fur that's two months old in your arms, but animals mature much sooner than humans do. Your veterinarian can advise you about the right time to have your animal spayed or neutered, taking into account the animal, her health, and her environment. If you're adopting an older animal who hasn't been neutered, check with your veterinarian about what's in the animal's best interest.

Spaying and neutering do involve surgery, even if it is fairly routine surgery, and that always brings with it some level of risk. Find out from your veterinarian what time of day your companion will be in surgery, and hold your animal in prayer during that time. You may want to visualize God's presence surrounding your companion and her doctor and nurse during the operation. God's presence can take many forms: a gentle cloud, a vibrantly colored light, God's "hands" surrounding the operation, or anything else that comes to you. You may also find simple and well-known prayers, such as Psalm 23, or the Lord's Prayer to be helpful. An anonymous tenth-century Celtic prayer might help you pray at this time:

The Lord Jesus Christ be near you to defend you,
within you to refresh you,
around you to protect you,
before you to guide you,
behind you to justify you,
above you to bless you.[56]

This kind of prayer can be used any time your animal needs surgery or procedures, or even just for routine vet visits. See the next chapter for suggestions on dealing with medications and procedures, and for suggestions about caring for your animal following surgery.

Mom Care

If you are planning on welcoming new life into this world, and you have the resources to care for the baby animals, or you have homes to send them to, caring for the mother animal becomes part of your covenant with your companion. Many of the saints seemed to have a special fondness for mother animals. In one particularly charming story sixth-century Pisentius, the Bishop of Qift, was approached by a peasant who wanted the bishop to bless his cow, which Pisentius did by making the sign of the cross on the cow's pregnant belly. When the calf was born she, too, bore the sign of the cross that the bishop had marked on her mother. The cross was a white as wool or snow, the story says, indicating great holiness.

Female animals, just like human animals, need special care during pregnancy. If your animal has health problems, check with your veterinarian before considering the possibility of pregnancy. Each species of animal has particular needs in pregnancy which can be researched online, in books, or by asking your veterinarian. Some of the basics that you'll probably have to consider include the following.

- Habitat: Your animal's habitat may need to be changed or adjusted during this period. Some animals, particularly guinea pigs or hamsters, may need to be moved to a quiet place away from noise and stresses. The temperature of the habitat might become an issue during pregnancy. Other animals will want to nest, particularly during the final stages of pregnancy, and you can help by providing towels or other safe materials that would make a comfortable and safe nest for the mom and newborns.
- Food: The mother animal's diet may need to be adjusted during pregnancy and after the birth; she's eating for more than one now. Your companion may need a richer diet that provides nutrients for her unborn babies, or she'll need a diet following birth that helps her produce the food the newborns need to stay healthy and grow. Talk to your veterinarian about what kind of diet is most appropriate for your particular animal.

- Other animals: The pregnant female may need to be kept away from other animals for her own safety, and sometimes for the safety of her newborns. Male guinea pigs, hamsters, and rabbits may be very dangerous for the baby animals, and they may also impregnate the female again right after the birth. In the case of dogs and cats you may want to keep your female away from public places where she could encounter other animals who might be ill. Even if your cat is an indoor/outdoor cat, you may want to keep the cat indoors, especially in the final stages of pregnancy, so you can provide a warm and safe place for the birth of the kittens.
- Medical Care: Talk with your veterinarian about what kind of pre-natal care your animal may need. Vaccinations are not generally given to animals during their pregnancies, but your vet can advise you about the effects or problems posed by any medicines your animal may be on already.
- Labor: Learn about what a normal delivery looks like for your particular animal, and what the signs of distress are. Talk to your veterinarian in advance about arrangements for care in the event that you think your animal is having problems with her delivery.

You might also consider blessing your pregnant animal. A simple prayer of blessing follows. You can say it while placing your hands on the animal herself, or on her habitat.

Creator God,

We thank you for the gift of new life

that your creature _____ now carries.

Be with her on this journey.

Nourish her and the new life that grows within her.

Give her strength when the birthing time is upon her.

Bless her and those she brings forth,

all of them your beloved creatures.

Amen.

—D.K.F.

Welcoming New Life

"As soon as convenient after the birth of a child, or after receiving a child by adoption," reads the Episcopal *Book of Common Prayer*, "the parents, along with other members of the family, should come to the church to be welcomed by the congregation and to give thanks to Almighty God."[57] I've never seen this service called "A Thanksgiving for the Birth of Adoption of a Child" used in any church of which I've been part, but it includes many wonderful prayers for the family and child, as well as affirmations of the responsibilities and joys that come with birth or adoption. There is a similar one found in the *United Methodist Book of Worship*. While the following prayer is written acknowledging the adoption of human children, it speaks to me as well of the covenant we're to make with the baby animals entrusted to our care:

Dear Friends: It has pleased God our Heavenly Father to answer the earnest prayers of N. [and N.], member(s) of this Christian family, for the gift of a child. I bid you join with them [and with N. (and NN.), who now has a new brother (sister)] in offering heartfelt thanks for the joyful and solemn responsibility which is theirs by the coming of N. to be a member of their family.[58]

The presence of newborn animals is a great joy—a time to wonder— and it is also a time to acknowledge the responsibilities we have for these new members of the household, even if they will be in the home only on a temporary basis. We are called to care for them as God would, just like we care for their parent or parents.

I haven't found any stories about newborn baby animals in the stories of the ancient desert dwellers or Celts, but there are many stories of young animals who needed help from one saint or another; these animals seemed to pull on their heartstrings. Bartholomew, a twelfth-century monk, lived as a hermit on the island of Inner Farne, a place full of birds and ducks. A duck came running up to him one day. The duck was most distressed, and kept tugging on Bartholomew's robe. At first he didn't understand what she wanted, but finally he realized that she wanted him to follow her, which he did. The duck took him to a cliff with a deep fissure, and motioned to him to look down. Looking down Bartholomew spotted a baby duckling, clinging to the cliff with its wings. He climbed down and brought the duckling back up and returned it to its mother, who seemed to thank him. This is, in many ways, the kind of respect, service, and care that we owe to the young ones that our animals birth.

Newborns and their mother need a habitat or room that is comfortable and safe, where they can be isolated from other animals, and where food and water are easily available to the mother animal. Their mother will probably be the primary caretaker for a while, feeding the young and teaching them the skills they need. Often newborn animals should be largely free of human contact for a period of time, unless medical intervention is necessary; baby animals need the attention of their mother, and human interaction may be hurtful to the very young. Check with your veterinarian if you're not sure about when handling newborns is permissible.

Eventually we will need to help wean the newborns from eating what their mother provides. Depending on the animal you may need to be involved in things like housebreaking. If you have puppies or kittens, ensure that proper veterinary care is provided at the right time. And one of the very special joys of new animals is playing with them when they are ready for human contact. The play socializes them so that human contact is comfortable, and it is educational for the baby animals. It is also one of the most entertaining ways to spend time that I can think of. I can spend hours watching baby animals chase items or each other, wrestle with toys or their siblings, climb, leap, and bounce around; the laughter at their antics is good for the soul.

Be sure, as well, to bless the new animals, recognizing them as gifts and beloved creatures of God. The following blessing can be used any time after the new animals are ready for a little human company. When you can bless them without causing the mother animal anxiety or the newborns harm, consider gathering around their habitat and offering them the following blessing:

Holy Spirit, Breath of Life, bless all these newborns with health of body and strength of spirit, so that they may bring joy and love to all who are blessed with their companionship. Amen.[59]

—Anthony Chiffolo

Follow the blessing with a pat for each animal if that is comfortable for mama and babies. If you are comfortable doing so, you might also want to make the sign of the cross over the animals, as the bishop Pisentius did in the early story about blessing the cow. This marks the animals as Christ's own.

All of this is part of the covenant we have with the baby animals, as is the ongoing care of the animals as they grow. If you plan to keep the newborns in your own home, go ahead and covenant with them, as you did with the mother. Otherwise make sure that they have a good home to go to when they are old enough. Ask prospective caregivers some of the same questions you considered when you brought the mother animal into your home. Can those in the prospective home afford to care for the animal? Do they know how to care for her, or are they willing to learn? Do the new "parents" have a veterinarian already? Don't be afraid to be proactive about inviting people who you think would take good care of an animal to think about bringing one of the newborns into their home. A friend of mine has lived with a wonderful German shepherd for nearly a decade now because friends of his called him and asked if he wanted a puppy to love.

CHAPTER ELEVEN

Caring for the Sick

✑✑✑✑

When the crowds found out about it, they followed him; and he
welcomed them, and spoke to them about the kingdom of God,
and healed those who needed to be cured.

—Luke 9:11

*I*t was said that Godric, who at age forty took up a life of asceticism back in the twelfth century, roamed around the countryside taking care of animals who were hurt. If he found an animal dying in the cold he would tuck the animal under his armpit until it warmed up. He searched through hedges and patches of brambles, and whenever he found an animal who was hurt or dying he used whatever medical skills he had to care for the creature. He even went so far as to free animals from traps when he found them, much to the consternation of the local hunters. Godric, like so many other saints, felt a deep sense of kinship with animals who were sick, injured, or trapped.

One of the most difficult aspects of living with animals we love is knowing that they—like we—will fall ill at times, sometimes seriously ill. Keep a basic book around that describes health concerns for whatever kind of animal you have, with simple first-aid suggestions, as well as descriptions of conditions that require immediate veterinary care. (Check with your veterinarian for a good book if you're not sure what book to trust.)

We can't prevent every illness in our animals, any more than we can for ourselves, but we can bring them for their routine physical exams each year, a procedure that can help prevent health problems, or catch them early. "Jesus came as our healer that we 'may have life, and have it abundantly,'" says the monastic rule (or instructions for living) of the Anglican Society of Saint John the Evangelist in Cambridge, Massachusetts. "We show our lack of faith in him if we diminish that abundance through neglect. . . . Health of mind, body, and spirit is a priceless gift of the Creation which we are to cherish in wonder and thankfulness."[60] And cherishing the gift of health means that we safeguard it through regular preventative care and checkups by our companion's veterinarian. Making time for and giving the financial resources required for those annual exams is an outward expression of our love for our companions as a part of God's creation. Here's a short prayer you might use when taking your companion in for a routine physical.

Good Saint Francis, you loved all of God's creatures. To you they were your brothers and sisters. Help us to follow your example of treating every living thing with kindness. Saint Francis, patron saint of animals, watch over my pet and keep my companion safe and healthy. Amen.

—traditional prayer[61]

With the development of more sophisticated care for animals, the money questions become major sometimes, especially when it comes to extra tests or procedures. For some people pet insurance will be helpful, though not all veterinarians accept it. But if your vet accepts insurance, and finances are tight, this may be a good option for you. Your vet may also be able to help you with costs if you let him or her know up front that this is an issue. Some veterinarians offer senior citizen discounts (when you're the senior, not your companion!), and many of them will also work out a payment plan with you if that's needed. At the veterinarian's office where my cat got her echocardiogram recently the pamphlet describing services at the office included this statement: "If you have some financial difficulty, please let us know in advance so that a reasonable alternative can be worked out. Lack of money should not prevent your pet from receiving needed medical care." Most good veterinarians who care about the patients they treat will echo that sentiment and do what they can to help you work out the finances. Check, too, with your local humane society; they may be able to provide you with low-cost health care or refer you to someone who can.

Checking the Lion's Paw

There will be a time for most of us, however, when more than routine medical care is required. Among the many stories of the Desert Fathers and the Celtic saints with animals, healing stories, like the one about Jerome and the lion, are among the most common. One night Jerome, a fourth-century priest who produced the first standard Latin translation of the Bible, sat in the monastery yard reading from Scripture, and a lion wandered in. Most of his fellow brothers fled in terror, but Jerome noticed that the lion was only walking on three legs and was holding the fourth up off the ground. Jerome went over to the lion to see what was wrong, and the lion held out his injured paw for Jerome to see. The man, seeing the injury, called on his fellow brothers to come pull the thorn from the lion's paw, wash the paw, and apply the necessary medicines. They did as Jerome asked, and the paw healed quickly. The lion was so grateful that he chose to live at the monastery for the remainder of his life.

I suspect stories of healing animals are common in the early Christian literature because it is in healing the animals that the Desert Fathers and saints could imitate the compassion of Jesus most closely. Jesus' ability to be present to those in need of healing seems inexhaustible at times. The Gospels include stories of Jesus healing the multitudes, as well as individuals who approach him for attention and care. People with illnesses and disabilities often evoke Jesus' sympathy and a merciful response. "If you choose, you can make me clean," a leper says to Jesus (Mark 1:40). "Moved with pity," Mark tells us, "Jesus stretched out his hand and touched him, and said to him, 'I do choose.'" Just as was true for the early Christians, perhaps it is in this area of illness and our responses to it that we, too, can be most Christ-like in our compassion for the animals who live with us.

Figuring out what is wrong with your companion requires some of the same attention that Jerome showed to the lion. I've yet to meet a dog, cat, gerbil, or bird who could use words to tell me that it wasn't well, but an animal's actions often indicate that she's not feeling up to par. Like Jerome we have to pay attention; part of our covenant with our companions is to know them well enough to notice small changes. You won't be able to detect every illness every time, but you know your companion best, and in many cases, you're the most likely person to detect small changes that signal the need for medical attention. Signs of illness might include changes in eating habits, behavioral changes, changes in elimination habits, hiding for extended periods of time, or changes in grooming behaviors. Any change, however, that appears suddenly and seems out of the ordinary, is worth asking your veterinarian about.

Prayer for the Sick

O God,
the strength of the weak and the comfort of sufferers,
mercifully hear our prayers
and grant to your servant N.,
the help of your power,
that his/her sickness may be turned into health
and our sorrow into joy;
through Jesus Christ. Amen.[62]

The Blessing of the Sick

Our Lord Jesus Christ be with you to defend you,
within you to keep you,
before you to lead you,
beside you to guard you,
and above you to bless you.
Amen.[63]

Home Care

Before my husband and I were married he had a wonderful dog, Max, who required regular medicines each day; all you had to do to get a pill down Max was to wrap it in a piece of bread, and he gobbled it right down. My cat Codi, now of blessed memory, on the other hand also had to take a daily medicine, and the task of getting pills down his throat was a good bit more onerous than getting a pill down Max.

Medical intervention for companion animals these days often involves regular treatment at home. Some regimes are short-term, as in after a routine surgery or other procedure; at other times you may need to treat your companion for the rest of his life. Part of our covenant is being willing and able to provide this kind of care. Daily medical routines are not always pleasant moments for our companions; sometimes they're more like wrestling matches than anything else. I swear that Stripe, our cat with heart problems, knows that I'm getting her medicine ready even when she's upstairs and I'm downstairs; she's always hiding by the time I get upstairs with her medicine.

There are no easy ways to make medical routines completely easy for animals, but we can approach them as ministry, with the recognition that we are God's hands, and perhaps lessen the strain of the event. Take a few moments to pray over the medicine or whatever equipment is involved in caring for your animal; thank God and all the hands that made the medicines, equipment, or procedures that are helping your companion. You might even use this moment to hold up to God other animals in the world, known or unknown to you, who are dealing with the same kind of illness. Take one more moment to imagine God's love surrounding your companion, working in concert with you to bring about whatever healing or cure is possible.

When you have your animal with you, and are ready to administer the medicine or procedure, take a moment (if you can do so without making matters worse for your companion) to lay your hands on him. Perhaps it would be helpful to hold or pet the animal and let him know that you love him and are trying to help. I spend a few minutes holding Stripe each day before I give her the heart medicines, petting her, and speaking to her quietly. Often I apologize to her for doing something she doesn't understand. At first she resisted being held, and did everything she could to get away from the medicines. Over several week's time, however, she seemed to sense that I wasn't going to hurt her, and she has allowed me to hold her even after administering the medicine—mostly, I suspect, to get another apology out of me.

No matter what your medical regime, think of it as a way of being the presence of the compassionate Christ for your animal. What kind of prayer or ritual will help you approach the treatment in the most compassionate and gentle way? What will make the procedure easiest for the animal? God is present in the medicines and procedures that are helping your animal; find ways of acknowledging that and letting God's love flow from your own hands to your companion in some way.

A Blessing for Medicine

Lord, whose almighty healing power is principally exercised through human acts and physical matter, as when your Son anointed the eyes of the blind man with spittle and clay that his sight might be restored, we ask you to bless these material things dedicated to N.'s healing (or alleviation of pain). Through the same Christ our Lord. Amen.[64]

—Sean Finnegan

Hospital Visits

When your companion has to stay at the vet practice for a period of time following a surgery, or to receive a treatment you can't effect at home, make time as often as possible to go visit, unless your veterinarian advises otherwise. Your animal is undoubtedly scared and less comfortable than he would be at home, and your presence will not only be welcome, but may well contribute to the animal's healing ability. Any good veterinarian will provide visiting hours and a space for you to spend time with your companion while she's at the clinic. Depending on your animal's health and abilities, spend time just petting or talking with her, or perhaps playing with her if your veterinarian says this is okay. Take a few moments to pray for your animal as well, perhaps using one of the prayers for the sick (see page 138).

While you are visiting with your companion, you might also take a moment to pray for those who are caring for her. Thank God for the clinic staff in your own words, or use this simple prayer.

O Lord Jesus Christ, who went about doing good and healing all kinds of sickness: give strength, wisdom and gentleness to all your ministering servants, that they may not only heal but bless, and shine as lamps of hope in the darkest hours of distress and fear. Amen.

—Church Missionary Society, 1899, adapted[65]

What Are the Limits?

One of the most difficult decisions to make, in caring for the animals we love, is how much testing and medical intervention is appropriate. We have so many more options in these areas than we did even ten years ago. That sometimes leaves us feeling that as conscientious and compassionate people, we must try every test, surgery, or procedure, even when we can't afford it. At times we also confuse being conscientious with not wanting to let go of the life of an animal we love, something that any of us are loath to do.

When our veterinarian first discovered that our cat, Stripe, had an extremely rapid heartbeat, my husband and I began to explore the options. Blood tests and an EKG were relatively simple procedures, ones that we thought should be done. When neither of them told us anything helpful, we were faced with taking Stripe for an echocardiogram. After considering this for some time, we decided that this also seemed reasonable, and we took her for that procedure. From that test we learned that she has a thickening heart muscle, a heart disease that is likely to shorten her life. She gets daily heart medicines now, and so far she is still active and healthy, and we are committed to caring for her at this level, knowing that we may not have her with us nearly as long as we would like. This is as much as can be done for her at this point, but we live with her knowing that we will probably have to make more decisions about medical procedures in the future, and we are agreed that we will continue to treat her as long as she has a good quality of life, is comfortable and pain-free, but the fact is that her heart muscle is thickening, and the medicine she takes for it will probably affect her kidneys in the long run. Neither of us wishes to prolong her suffering when her heart can no longer sustain her life without major intervention.

There are no hard and fast rules about the limits any of us will place on medical testing and care, but asking yourself the following questions may help bring some clarity:

- Will the treatment be invasive, and, if so, how will that affect the animal in the short and long term?
- Does the procedure or surgery stand a good chance of providing important information or extending a good quality of life for the animal?
- What will be the financial costs of the various options being considered? For some this will not be an issue, but for others the costs may be prohibitive. Some of the financial options listed earlier in this chapter may be helpful, but most of us need to recognize that there are limits to the amount of money we can spend. This is especially important when expensive procedures are only prolonging a poor quality of life for an animal we don't want to lose. Regardless of the circumstances, we must provide for the animal as best we can, but our covenant does not include going into bankruptcy for an animal's heart transplant.
- If the procedure continues to extend the life of an animal that has been struggling for a time, when will enough be enough for your companion? For you? Are you keeping your companion alive for her own sake, or for yours?

These are difficult questions, and none of them have right or wrong answers. Often all of those who live with and care for an animal need to be in conversation about these questions; thinking about them before you're in a crisis can be enormously helpful. Praying about the difficult choices is also important. If they're helpful, use some of the prayers below to begin your conversation with God, and then listen in silence for a period of time and see if you sense God guiding you in a particular direction. Talk with others you trust, and particularly with your veterinarian about the options as well; God often speaks to us through those around us.

In a Time of Difficult Decision

Lord of all wisdom and source of all life, we come before you as we struggle with decisions about life and death that rightly belong to you alone. We confess that we act with uncertainty now. Give us your help, and guide us, merciful God, in your loving concern for N. who lives in grave illness; through Jesus Christ our Lord. Amen.[66]

At the Limits of Our Power to Help

O Lord, we are at the limits of our power to help. For what we have left undone, forgive us. For what you have helped us to do, we thank you. For what must be done by others, lend your strength. Now shelter us in your peace which passes our understanding. Amen.[67]

Emergency!

I was in my veterinarian's office one day when a sobbing woman came in with her dog in her arms. He had been hit by a car, and she had rushed him to the vet's office hoping that he was still alive and could be helped. He was dead, and the clinic staff stopped everything to help and comfort her. These kinds of emergencies—whether due to an accident or a sudden change in health—are the kinds of events we dread. In the middle of them we're not likely to be very rational; all we're focused on is getting care for our companion, which is obviously the first priority. But when and if there is a moment, when your animal is being examined or is in surgery, take a moment to imagine your companion being held in God's caring hands, no matter what the outcome. I do this by imagining my animal surrounded by light, which is one of my favorite images of God, but use any imagery that makes sense to you.

Take a moment, too, to pray for those who are caring for your animal in this emergency.

God, Divine Healer,
our only source of health and hope,
Guide now the actions of those who care for N.:
May they bring all their knowledge and skill
to bear on N.'s care;
May their skillful hands do not only their work
but convey their deep care for him;
Give your healers energy and strength and stamina
as they seek to help and heal our beloved friend.
Amen.
—D.K.F.

CHAPTER TWELVE

And Now the End is Near

For now we see in a mirror, dimly, but then we will see face to face. Now I know only in part; then I will know fully, even as I have been fully known.
—1 Corinthians 13:12

Many years ago, before I traveled so often, I worked as a hospice volunteer. There are few moments as powerful as those spent sitting with the dying and their families and loved ones. When death is imminent there is little time for small talk, and all that is unimportant simply fades away. I considered it a privilege to be with people during these transitional times in their lives. This was a painful experience for many of them, but also it provided the gift of the time to say good-bye to those they loved if they chose to do so. We don't have a hospice movement for animals, and that is a shame. It could teach us about how to let go, and how to let death occur naturally and with as little pain as possible.

When we're faced with our animal's pending death we are often given black and white choices: to provide endless or protracted (costly) treatment or to euthanize right away. Many people find it difficult to make these choices. I suspect that if the hospice philosophy were more widely understood as a way to be with animals at the end that end-of-life decisions might be just a little less awful. What we need, however, is a way to make an animal comfortable, and to find ways of saying good-bye—both of which hospice promotes. The hospice philosophy is often the middle ground between endless treatment and euthanasia that can take into account the kind care of the animal and the human sadness at saying good-bye.

Since most domestic animals live a shorter number of years than humans we live with them knowing that the chances are very good that we'll have to deal with this someday, but knowing that it's coming and dealing with it are two different issues. No one is ever ready to make a decision to discontinue medical treatment or to euthanize an animal who is suffering; no one wants to say good-bye to a beloved friend. But there are times when discontinuing treatment or euthanizing an animal are the kindest things we can do.

Decisions are often difficult to make because colleagues or others in our communities don't understand the powerful relationships we have with our animals, two beings who have lived together for years, and who rely on each other for love, affection, and understanding. We do not always have the opportunity to say good-bye to an animal we love, but when we are able to do so, that time—sad as it is—can also be a gift. The pending death, and all the decisions surrounding it, is a momentous occasion, and there are ways to honor it with dignity.

Care at the End—A Hospice Approach

There comes a time with animals, as with humans, where medical intervention is no longer useful; when all it can do is prolong a poor quality of life a little bit longer. Hospice care for humans begins when treatment ends, when all that is left to do is to make our companions comfortable. Skilled nurses, social workers, chaplains, and others in hospice work attend to the patient's physical comfort, especially pain control, as well as helping the patient and her family with any tasks or needs that should be addressed before death. When used wisely and well, the time in hospice can help patients and families focus on saying good-bye. Adapting the hospice philosophy, we can try to provide much the same things for our companions: pain-free life while there is life to be had, in a comfortable, stress-free environment, using this time to say our own farewells.

When a person enters hospice care the staff usually helps any family or friends serving as caregivers to know what to expect. Ask your veterinarian for the same information; knowing what to expect as your animal's body begins to close down will help you feel less panicked as these natural processes begin. An animal near the end of her life will often be fairly quiet and inactive. Many times she will stop eating. Some animals will want to be alone; they'll curl up in a closet, under the bed, or someplace else that is comfortable, dark, and quiet. Other animals will want to be close to their humans, in the midst of activity, even if they're relatively quiet. Though it can be very painful to let your animal go off by herself when all you want to do is to be with her, try to respect her wishes as much as you can.

Provide whatever physical relief you can for your companion. Pay attention to the temperature of your animal's environment, and make sure it is comfortable. Provide food and water if your companion wants it, but don't force it on her. Maintain a quiet environment without lots of activity or stimulus. Approach your friend gently, and without expectations; your presence will be enough. Pet her, or talk quietly to her if that seems to be helpful, but allow her time to sleep as well. The goal is to let your animal have a quiet, dignified death if possible. In hospice for people everyone involved agrees to forego life-saving measures as death draws near; though it is very difficult to avoid these, once your animal is past help with medical care, resist trying extraordinary measures, especially ones your veterinarian says will probably be useless. As hard as it is, your companion's need for a peaceful death has to come first during this time.

During this period of watching and waiting you might consider talking about what you want to do with your animal's body after death, or what kind of funeral or memorial would be helpful. (Various options can be found in the next chapter.) Though talking about these matters can make death feel more real, talking about your love of the animal and how you want to honor that after her death can also be healing. I remember that when it was clear that my beloved cat Codi was not going to live more than a few days longer I went to our local plant nursery and bought a butterfly bush to mark what would be his grave. It was a very difficult trip, and I cried a great deal, but there was also something very healing about bringing home a plant that would attract butterflies to his gravesite later on.

If there are children in the house, be honest with them about what's going on, and help them understand that the animal's death is approaching. If they are old enough, involve them in helping to make decisions about what to do to memorialize their friend. Just like you, they may have a whole range of feelings, from anger to grief, about losing their companion. Be honest with them about your own feelings of sadness, grief, and anger, and let them know that whatever they are feeling is also okay. Give them time to talk about their feelings, to ask questions, and to express themselves. And give them the opportunity to watch and observe as their companions goes through the dying experience.

Vigiling

A friend of mine, Megory Anderson, is responsible for coining the wonderful word "vigiling." In her book *Sacred Dying* she talks about how to be with people who are dying, something that we have largely forgotten how to do in this culture where deaths take place in hospitals and out of our sight. One of the practices she recommends, as a result of her own extensive work with those who are dying, is the practice of vigiling, or sitting with the dying. Vigiling is the simple practice of preparing a space—physical and emotional—for those who are dying. It is about meeting their needs whenever possible, and about creating a quiet and gentle environment in which the dying can happen as peacefully as possible.

Before my husband and I were married, his elderly dog Max had arthritis and some skin problems. Max got medicines regularly for both, but a couple of months before he died it became clear that he was deteriorating. He had more difficulties with walking, and especially with climbing even a few steps. His skin disease grew noticeably worse, with some open wounds that attracted bugs. My husband did all he could to make Max comfortable in those last few months. Max spent a lot of time sleeping on his mat in the living room, and with the cat Kit. But as the days wore on we knew Max was at the end. The skin disease was becoming uncontrollable, and Max could hardly get off his mat to go outside. My husband made an appointment for him at the vet's office, knowing that it was likely that he would come home from that appointment without Max. That last night Max got a bath. It was a hot July evening, and Max had bugs burrowed into his skin once again. I took him outside and gently washed him to remove the bugs, and then brought him back inside for a towel-drying, which seemed to feel good to him. Max was, indeed, euthanized the next day, but at least his final night was a little more comfortable, and we got a chance to say good-bye in a very loving and hands-on way.

Vigils do not need to be complicated or a big production. A friend of mine tells a touching story of vigiling with her dog Nicki. Nicki had had a stroke and other problems; she was hardly even able to walk anymore. She was scheduled for a vet visit the next day, but it was clear that medical intervention was not likely to be helpful. Poor Nicki tried to turn over as she lay on the floor, but she couldn't even make her hind feet move with her. Sue placed a terrycloth bathrobe on one side of Nicki to help her stay still, and she, with the rest of the animals in her home present as well, read some prayers for the sick and the dying. And then she simply talked to Nicki for a while, telling Nicki how much she loved her and that she didn't have to hang on anymore. Nicki died that night, a peaceful and quiet death.

Vigiling with an animal at home can be as simple as sitting with her and telling her that you love her, or giving her a bath, holding her, or any number of other things that seem to be of comfort to your companion. Let each member of the household have a chance to say good-bye and don't forget to include other animals in the house if they are close to the one who is dying. Animals know what is going on, and mourn the loss of companions as much as humans do. Speak to your companion from your own heart, or if you find it more helpful, use one or more of the prayers at the end of this chapter.

Vigils in the Vet's Office

Sometimes our animals are at the vet's office when medical treatment becomes unhelpful and is terminated. If your companion is not in discomfort or pain, and you wish, talk to your veterinarian about taking her home to die. If she is suffering, however, you may be asked to make a decision about euthanizing her, one of the most difficult decisions we have to make. Each of us will have to decide for ourselves if this is acceptable, but don't let yourself be rushed into this decision. If you don't wish to euthanize your companion, your vet may be able to help keep the animal comfortable until she dies. If you choose to euthanize her, spend some time with her beforehand, much as you would with a vigil at home. (Some veterinarians will also come to your home to euthanize your companion, saving your companion the stress of a vet visit if she is at home when the decision is made.) Hold her or pet her if this is comfortable for the animal. Take whatever time you need to say good-bye, and to tell your companion that you love her. You may want to bring a favorite blanket or some object that comforts your companion when you say good-bye. Don't let this last visit be rushed; you and other members of your household need time to say good-bye. If it is comfortable for your animal, pray over her, using some of the prayers at the end of this chapter.

If you are able to manage it, be present when your animal is euthanized. Let her last moments be ones where you are caressing her, and offering her comfort. When your companion is gone, you may wish to spend time with her body; a good veterinarian will not rush you out of the room, but give you time to grieve and be with your companion for a bit. Or, if you plan to bury your companion at home, you can bring your companion's body home and spend some time with it there. You may find it helpful to observe some sort of vigil after the death as well, whether at the vet's office or at home, much as humans sometimes have a wake for those who have died. Again, this doesn't need to be complicated, just heartfelt. Take the time you need to say good-bye, or to plan a memorial for your companion. Light a candle and sit with the body and pray over it for a while. Gather all those in the household and share stories of the animal's life. Try not to censor your ideas of what is acceptable at this time, and follow your instincts to do whatever you need to do to simply be with the body and get used to the idea of your companion's death.

Again, don't forget about the other animals in the house at this time. Animals grieve when their companions die. When my husband's dog Max died, the cat, who always slept with Max, wouldn't come into the house for a couple of weeks. If you're able, let other animals in the house see the body so they know what has happened. Codi had to be euthanized in the vet's office after being there for many days, and Gabi, the other cat in the house, was agitated the whole time. When Codi was gone my veterinarian suggested that I take him home in his cat-coffin and let the other cat in the house, Gabi, see that he was dead. Gabi came over and took one sniff of Codi and ran upstairs, but she knew what had happened, and she was much calmer after that.

Seeing an animal through death is always difficult; most of us need companionship during this time. Don't forget to take care of yourself or let others help you do that while you're caring for your companion. You and any others in the household who love the dying animal need support from others who understand how important your animal companion is to you. Let friends and loved ones help you through these times; if your priest or minister seems sympathetic, don't be afraid to call on them for help as well.

Creator God
in whose sight
all life is holy
and before whom
all the creatures
of the earth
are remembered;
bless this creature, (Name),

with your Holy Spirit
and grant him/her with us
a share in
your eternal kingdom.
Amen.

Dear God
you have enlivened
all the creatures
of the earth
with your Spirit;
nothing dies
but is remembered by you
and nothing lives
without your grace;
bless this innocent creature, (Name),
and by your same Spirit
grant him/her and all your creatures
eternal life in your presence.
Amen.
—Andrew Linzey[68]

For People Watching at a Death

God of the dark night,
you were with Jesus praying in the garden,
you were with Jesus all the way to the cross
and through to the resurrection.
Help us to recognize you now, as we watch with N.,
and wait for what must happen;
help us through any bitterness and despair,
help us to accept our distress,
help us to remember that you care for us
and that in your will is our peace.[69]

Keep watch, dear Lord, with those who work, or watch, or weep this night,
and give your angels charge over those who sleep. Tend the sick, Lord Christ;
give rest to the weary, bless the dying, soothe the suffering, pity the afflicted,
shield the joyous; and all for your love's sake. Amen.
— The Book of Common Prayer

CHAPTER THIRTEEN

Rest in Peace

✧✧✧✧

For the fate of humans and the fate of animals is the same; as one dies, so dies the other. They all have the same breath, and humans have no advantage over the animals; for all is vanity. All go to one place; all are from the dust, and all turn to dust again. Who knows whether the human spirit goes upward and the spirit of animals goes downward to the earth?

—Ecclesiastes 3:19–21

*I*t was one of the most powerful rituals I've ever experienced. On All Saint's Day, in a Unitarian church in Syracuse, NY, everyone who entered was given the option of writing the names of loved ones who had died on leaves made of construction paper. Some people wrote the names of human friends and loved ones; many wrote the name of companion animals who no longer walked the earth. In the middle of the service we were all invited to bring those leaves up and hang them on a naked tree. The tree, which looked so dead and forlorn at the start of the service, was lit up with fall-colored leaves and with the names and memories of those we missed. What had been dead came alive, and there were few dry eyes in the congregation that morning.

The loss of our animal companions is always heart-breaking. Like Mary and Martha outside Lazarus' tomb, we grieve the loss of a being we love dearly; if we had the option of asking Christ to bring our companion back, we'd jump at the chance. And all the platitudes in the world don't help at this time.

I don't know what happens after we die; this is another of those Job-like moments for me when I have to admit that God is in many ways mysterious, and that I cannot know all of God's ways. But I believe that the same thing that happens to people happens to animals. Marcus Borg, in his excellent book *The Heart of Christianity*, writes: "We live in God. We move in God. We have our being in God. And when we die, we do not die into nothingness; we die into God."[70] My own image for this is that we all die into the arms of the God who loves us forever. Knowing that our animal is in the arms of God (where you and I will be someday) may comfort us a little at the moment, but truthfully, right when an animal dies we'd rather have her in our own arms. Knowing that her struggle is over or that she is at peace is also small comfort in the first days after a death, though it will be a little later. At the time of death, it is natural to simply want your companion back.

These days are ones for being gentle with yourself, physically, emotionally, and spiritually. Grief, with its anger and sadness all rolled up together, is powerful and physically exhausting. You may find that you're too tired, or even too angry to pray, and that's okay. If you have supportive friends or family, let others do the praying for you during these first days of grieving; God knows what is in your heart. If you're angry with God, that's also fine; God can take it.

When Codi died I was inconsolable for days. All I could do was cry. Marley, the man who is now my husband, sat with me much of the time and let me cry, or tell stories of Codi, or whatever I needed to do. After some hours of this I suddenly realized I was hungry; what I wanted most was a grilled cheese sandwich, one of my favorite comfort foods. Marley went to the store for me, bought some cheese, and came back and made me the sandwich. Let those around you help you in some of the same ways. This is a time to tell stories, to weep or be angry; it is also a time to let others help take care of you physically—to feed you and be God's compassionate presence for you.

Final Options

In the midst of all of these feelings, decisions about your companion's body need to be made. Think about this ahead of time if you can, so that you don't have to consider all these options in the midst of deep grief. There are several possibilities to consider.

Home burial: This is a good option if you want your animal's remains close by, and you don't expect to move. It is legal in most urban and rural areas these days, but you may want to check with your local authorities. In our backyard we have buried the bodies of various animals under the quince tree, and there is some sense of peace in knowing that there are all together in one place. Burying an animal in your own yard also allows the opportunity for a memorial of some sort—a plant or statue, perhaps, that marks the gravesite.

Pet Cemeteries and Crematories: In recent years more pet cemeteries have appeared. They offer both burial and cremation services for your animal, and may offer many of the other services that funeral homes offer for people. Visit www.iaopc.com (International Association of Pet Cemeteries and Crematories) to find facilities in your area, or check with your local humane society or veterinarian. Pet cemeteries may also be listed in the phone book.

With pet cemeteries you will also have to make decisions about whether you want your animal buried in a mass grave with other animals or buried individually; the second option is more expensive. The same is true for cremation; mass cremations are less expensive than individual ones. If you want to be sure that the ashes you receive are those of your animal alone, be sure to be clear about this. You will probably be given options of coffins or urns, as well as memorial markers. There are no right or wrong decisions in these areas. All of these are fine if you would like them, but choosing not to spend lots of money on these options does not mean you don't love your companion.

If you choose to have your animal cremated, and you wish to keep the ashes with you, you can select an urn or other container for the ashes that is meaningful for you. If you choose to scatter the ashes someplace meaningful, you can use the container supplied by the crematory for the short term.

The Funeral or Memorial

Whether you bury the body of your companion, or have him cremated, a funeral service or memorial service can be enormously healing. While these services bring home the finality of death once again, they also provide a way of honoring the life of your companion, and of saying good-bye. If burial is chosen then the service must be held within a few days of the death, or arrangements should be made to prevent the body from decomposing. When cremation is chosen scattering the ashes can be done at any time that feels appropriate.

As you think about the service, decide if you are able to lead it, or if you want to invite someone else to do this. When Codi died I found that my grief was simply too deep for me to speak at his funeral. As the awareness of the bond between humans and animals has deepened, more and more clergy are comfortable being asked to help with funerals for animal companions; but friends and household members can also lead whatever service you've planned. If the animal companion was part of a household, invite all the members to participate. Children often want to be part of the process of bury-ing a companion, or to help with scattering the ashes. Ask everyone if there is something special they would like to say or do to honor the animal, or if there is some item that was important to the animal that should be buried with him.

If you choose to bury your companion, dig the hole in advance, and then assemble all the participants around the gravesite. Use whichever prayers seem appropriate (some are included at the end of this chapter) and provide time for everyone to share a story, memory, or something else about the animal if they wish. If some-one wants to be silent, that's okay too. When the brief service is over, lower the animal into the grave along with any memento or object that was important to the animal. I buried Codi with his favorite blanket filled with catnip. Ask those assembled to help place some of the dirt back into the hole. If you have a memorial ready—perhaps a plant, a cross, or a statue of some sort—you can plant or place that as you fill the grave. You may wish to conclude the service with some silence. A time of celebration for the life of this particular animal is also appropriate if you wish. Much as we do for humans who have died, a reception with some time to talk and share more memories after the burial may be helpful.

The sequence can be much the same for the scattering of ashes, except that you can do this whenever it is most appropriate. You might choose to scatter the ashes someplace that was special to the animal, or a place where you and the animal spent time together. You may also choose to keep the ashes in an urn, rather than scatter them. Gather those who are participating together, and take time to pray and share memories and stories as you wish, and then, if you are scattering the ashes, you may invite others to help. If you are scattering them or burying them in your own yard, you can also place any memorials at this time. As with the burial, conclude with some silence, and/or with a time for celebrating your animal's life.

Prayers for Funerals and Memorial Services

I have provided a few options for prayers below, as well as one short service. Sometimes all we can manage is a short prayer and a lot of silence. Other times a more developed service is helpful. Use whichever seems most appropriate to your circumstances. Adjust the words as needed for use by groups or by an individual.

N., our companion in faith and brother/sister in Christ,
we entrust you to God.
Go forth from this world:
in the love of God who created you;
in the mercy of Jesus Christ who died for you;
in the power of the Holy Spirit who strengthens you,
at one with all the faithful, living and departed.
May you rest in peace and rise in the glory of your eternal home,
Where grief and misery are banished, and light and joy abide.
Amen.[71]

In sure and certain hope of the resurrection to eternal life
through our Lord Jesus Christ, we commit to Almighty God
our *brother N.*, and we commit *his* body to the ground [or to the
deep or the elements or its resting place]; earth to earth, ashes
to ashes, dust to dust. The Lord bless *him* and keep *him*, the Lord
make his face to shine upon *him* and be gracious to *him*, the Lord
life up his countenance upon *him* and give *him* peace. Amen.[72]

—*The Book of Common Prayer*

Lord God,
to those who have never had a pet
this prayer will sound strange,
but to You, Lord of All Life and Creator of All Creatures,
it will be understandable.
My heart is heavy
as I face the loss in death of my beloved _____
who was so much a part of my life.

This pet made my life more enjoyable
and gave me cause to laugh
and to find joy in his/her company.
I remember the fidelity and loyalty of this pet
and will miss his/her being with me.
From him/her I learned many lessons
such as the quality of naturalness
and the unembarrassed request for affection.
In caring for his/her daily needs,
I was taken up and out of my own self-needs
and thus learned to service another.

May the death of this creature of Yours
remind me that death comes to all of us,
animal and human,
and that it is the natural passage for all life.
May _____ sleep on
in an eternal slumber in Your godly care
as all creation awaits the fullness of liberation.
Amen.

—Edward Hays[73]

In Wisdom You Made Them
Marking the Death of a Pet

ᴈᴈᴈᴈ

Leader:	The Lord be with you!
All:	And also with you!
Leader:	O Lord, how manifold are your works; in wisdom you have made them all.
All:	The earth is full of your creatures; they look to you to give them their food in due season.
Leader:	When you open your hand, they are filled with good things; when you send forth your spirit, they are created.
All:	When you take away their breath, they die and return to their dust. (Psalm 104:24, 27–29)
Leader:	To God, who in every time and season cares for the earth and all its creatures,
All:	Be glory and honor, now and forever!

Leader: (addressing the community) One of the ways we are sustained in God's great love is through special relationships with pets. On this occasion, we gather to celebrate the life of _____. What memories will we share on this day?

Time is allowed for participants to share memories of the deceased pet's life. When the sharing has concluded the rite continues.

Leader: With what memento(s) will we continue to hold _____ in our hearts?

Time is allowed for a sharing mementos, such as photographs, tags or collars, and so forth. When the mementos have been shared, the rite continues.

Leader: Let us pray.

We give thanks, O God, for the gift of _____'s life and his/her presence in our lives. Console us in our loss and, in time, make our memories of _____ a source of comfort. Give us courage to entrust _____ to your tender care, knowing that, in every time and season, you use the cycles of life and death, joy and sorrow, beginnings and endings to renew your creation and restore all creation to you.

All: In the name of Christ, we pray. Amen.

Leader: The peace of the Lord be with you always!
All: And also with you!

The rite concludes with the sharing of the peace.
                    —Linda Henke[74]

A Few Last Words

As St. Francis, well-known for his love of the animals, was walking along one day, he stopped to preach a sermon to the birds.

"My little bird sisters," he said to them, "you owe a great deal to God your Creator, and always and everywhere you should praise him because he has given you a twofold and a threefold covering. Then he has given you the freedom to fly anywhere; and he preserved your seed in Noah's ark so that your species would not disappear from the earth. You are also indebted to him for the element of air that he has assigned to you. Besides this, you do not sow and you do not reap, and God feeds you and gives you the rivers and springs for you to drink from. He gives you the mountains and valleys for your refuge and the tall trees in which to make your nests. . . . Therefore, my little sisters, beware of the sin of ingratitude, but always strive to praise God."[75]

Francis's words to the birds, however, came long before humans began polluting the earth on a grand scale. In the past few decades scientists and others have made us much more aware of how humans have limited or destroyed the habitats, the air, and the water, a move that affects not only humans but the animals as well. The animals may have less reason to thank God today than they did in St. Francis's day.

The process of researching and writing this book has forced me to look at many questions that I have carefully avoided in the past. In the process of learning more about the mass farming of animals, the use of animals in laboratories, and other like questions, I have had to make some substantial changes in my own life. The more I wrote, the more I realized that the ramifications of what I was saying were larger than what appears on each page of this book. Each of us as Christians will need to make decisions about what part we are willing to play in the treatment of animals in this world, and there are no hard and fast answers that I can give you. I do believe that there is reason for hope, that some industries are becoming more aware of animals as sentient beings that should not be abused. Many of us are also becoming more aware of ways we can help the wild animals who live around us. A friend of mine, for instance, feeds the wild birds except when it is time for them to migrate. But it would be wrong for me to deny that the needless pain inflicted on many animals in this world does not sadden and disturb me. It is my deepest hope that in reading this book and learning to live in covenant with your companion animals that you will also begin to ask yourself questions and educate yourself about the other animals in the world, and your responsibility for the way they live and die. These are not small matters; they have as much to do with the state of our own souls and our relationship with God as they do with the quality of the life of animals entrusted to our care. God bless you in your journeys.

ACKNOWLEDGMENTS

No book is written in isolation, and it is an author's privilege and duty to thank those who—like midwives—help birth the new creation. An enormous thank-you goes to Dr. Charles Cook and the staff at the Episcopal Theological Seminary of the Southwest for granting me a two-week fellowship in Austin, Texas, to work on this book. Nancy Busby, at ETSS, provided so beautifully for the four of us who were "fellows" in Fall 2005 that I was able to spend two weeks on research and writing with nothing else to worry about. Dr. Alan Gregory provided stimulating conversation, and some important questions that helped shape the manuscript. Rob Cogswell and Mikail McIntosh-Doty and the rest of the library staff at ETSS found everything I could possibly have needed and more.

I am also indebted to those who read parts or all of this manuscript looking for errors and omissions; any that still exist are solely my fault. The Rev. Mary Earle, the Rev. Anne Kitch, and Dr. Ron Long were most helpful as readers. Megory Anderson, whose work on death and dying inspires me, deserves thanks for her careful reading of my material in this area, and for helpful suggestions. Jon Sweeney, a long-time friend, has been as good an editor as he has been a friend, and I'm grateful for his enthusiasm for the project and his willingness to help me think clearly when I got confused. Linda

Roghaar, my agent, was also passionate about this book, and I am grateful for her enthusiasm and help in placing it.

Finally, I am grateful to my husband, Marley, for helping me think about the material in this book, for listening to my garbled conversation as I thought through various sections, and for his loving support that has allowed me to write full–time. I am equally grateful to him that he didn't even so much as wince when I suggested we add a dog to all the cats in our household. I'm thankful to my stepson, Christian, as well for being willing to experiment with some of the material in this book, allowing me to see how it worked for a ten-year-old.

And perhaps most of all, I have to thank the animals who have lived with me over the last fifty–plus years. There are more of them than I can count—cats, dogs, gerbils, guinea pigs, and parakeets—and each has been my teacher in his or her own way.

APPENDIX

The Feast of St. Francis,
or The Blessing of the Animals

⁂

Congregations in many denominations today are offering "The Blessing of the Animals" as a service, usually around the time of St. Francis's feast day, October 4th. This time of year often works not only because of the feast day, but because the weather is usually still pleasant enough to have a service outside. There is no reason, however, why the service needs to be held outside. I have talked to pastors in some congregations who do an indoor service, or a blessing even in the context of regular Sunday worship or at a Christmas service, without any difficulties. If you're going to do an indoor service, or if you're forced indoors due to the weather, just be sure to have some folks assigned to clean up if need be. Accidents happen less often than most people expect, and animals tend to quiet down once the service gets started. Whether you plan to hold the service indoors or outdoors, stress the importance of bringing animals either on leads or in crates or other carrying devices, both for the sake of some level of calm and for the safety of all the animals themselves.

So many congregations now offer these blessing services that it is easy to find worship material on the Internet. Blessing services may also be found in various books such as Andrew Linzey's *Animal Rites*, and Anthony Chiffolo and Rayner Hesse's *We Thank You, God, for These*. Linzey's book, in particular, contains a wide variety of liturgies for congregational use not only for blessing services, but for healing, burial, and so on. But one size never fits all congregations. Below you'll find materials that you can mix and match to meet your own needs. (Please remember to cite the sources for these pieces in any service materials you put together. Sources are listed in the endnotes.)

Greeting/Openings:

1.

Leader: The Lord be with you!

All: And also with you!

Leader: O Lord, how manifold are your works!

All: You stretch out the heavens like a tent. You set the earth on its foundation. You make springs gush forth in the valleys and give drink to every animal.

Leader: You plant trees where birds may build their nests.

All: You cause the grass to grow for the cattle and plants for people to use. You open your hand and give all creatures their food in good season.

(*Psalm 104: 2, 5, 10-11, 14, 17, 24, 27-28*)[76]

—Linda Witte Henke

2.

One: We have come together to rejoice with God the creator at the wonderful creation around us.

O God, you love all things that exist: and despise none of the things which you have made, for you have made nothing you didn't love. You spare all things, for they are yours—O Lord who loves the living. For your immortal Spirit is in all things. (Wisdom 11:22ff.)

All: Let us sing to the Lord
a new song:
a song for all the creatures
of the earth.

One: Let us rejoice
in the goodness of God
shown in the beauty
of little things.

All: Let us marvel
        at the little creatures
        who are innocent
        in God's sight.

One: Let us extol
        God's handiwork
        in the complexity
        of their lives.

All: Let us not be haughty or proud
        too full of ourselves
        to praise the Lord
        of little things.

One: Let us rejoice
        in the other worlds
        sublime and mysterious
        that God has made:

All: the world of earthworms
        burrowing in the ground;

One: the world of skylarks
        soaring above us;

All: the world of foxes
         playing around their dens.

One: Let us hear
         the divine rejoicing
         throughout the whole earth:
         "the earth is mine
         and the fullness thereof." (Psalm 24:1)[77]

                  —Andrew Linzey

Prayers:

1.

"O God, enlarge within us the sense of fellowship with all living things, our brothers the animals to whom thou gavest the earth as their home in common with us.

We remember with shame that in the past we have exercised the high dominion of man with ruthless cruelty so that the voice of the earth, which should have gone up to thee in song, has been a groan of travail. May we realize that they live not for us alone but for themselves and for thee, and that they love the sweetness of life."
—St. Basil

2.

Lord, may we love all your creation,

all the earth and every grain of sand in it.

May we love every leaf, every ray of your light.

May we love the animals;

you have given them the rudiments of thought and joy untroubled.

Let us not trouble it;

let us not harass them,

let us not deprive them of their happiness,

let us not work against your intent.

For we acknowledge that unto you all that is like an ocean,

all is flowing and blending,

and that to withhold any measure of love from anything in
your universe

is to withhold that same measure from you. Amen.

　　　　—Fyodor Mikhailovich Dostoevsky (1821–1881)

3.

Blessed are you, living, loving God.

All creation praises you,

yet you have given the earth into our hands.

You made animals as our companions,

that in caring for them

we might learn to live and care
for all your creatures,
and find in them a sign of your grace.
As we fulfill this calling
may we draw close to you,
the giver of all life,
through Jesus Christ our Lord. Amen.[78]

4.

O Loving Father, we entreat Thee for our fellow creatures, the cattle,
the beasts of the field, and the fowls of the air; beseeching Thee
that, recognizing always our responsibility towards them, we may
learn from them to fulfill our appointed tasks in humility and trust-
fulness; through Jesus Christ our Lord.[79]

—Source unknown

5.

O Heavenly Father, Almighty and Eternal God, in times long past
You sent the friendly ravens to bring bread and meat to feed Your
prophet Elijah in his hour of need. And as You bade Your servant,
Noah, gather in the animals, each with his mate, within the shelter
of an Ark of Refuge, so now, we beseech You, send Your Holy Spirit
to inspire us with a vision of love, solicitude, and caring for this
wonderful world of living nature round us, bestowed on us in trust

by Your bountiful goodness. This we ask for the sake of Him Who once dwelt in the wilderness with the beasts of the wild, Jesus our Lord and Master.[80]

—Source unknown

6.

Lord, make us instruments of your peace.
Where there is hatred, let us sow love;
where there is injury, pardon;
where there is discord, union;
where there is doubt, faith;
where there is despair, hope;
where there is darkness, light;
where there is sadness, joy.
Grant that we may not so much seek to be consoled as to console;
to be understood as to understand;
to be loved as to love.
For it is in giving that we receive;
it is in pardoning that we are pardoned;
and it is in dying that we are born to eternal life.
Amen.

—attributed to St. Francis

Biblical readings:

Genesis 1:1-2, 20–25
Genesis 2:18–20
Genesis 9:8–17
Psalm 104:10–24
Isaiah 11:1–9
Matthew 18:10–14
Romans 8:18–23

Canticles:

12 A Song of Creation *Benedicite, omnia opera Domini*
Song of the Three Young Men, Daniel 3:35–65 (from the Apocrypha)

Invocation
Glorify the Lord, all you works of the Lord, *
praise him and highly exalt him for ever.
In the firmament of his power, glorify the Lord, *
praise him and highly exalt him for ever.

I. The Cosmic Order

Glorify the Lord, you angels and all powers of the Lord, *
O heavens and all waters above the heavens.
Sun and moon and stars of the sky, glorify the Lord, *
praise him and highly exalt him for ever.
Glorify the Lord, every shower of rain and fall of dew, *
all winds and fire and heat.
Winter and summer, glorify the Lord, *
praise him and highly exalt him for ever.
Glorify the Lord, O chill and cold, *
drops of dew and flakes of snow.
Frost and cold, ice and sleet, glorify the Lord, *
praise him and highly exalt him for ever.
Glorify the Lord, O nights and days, *
O shining light and enfolding dark.
Storm clouds and thunderbolts, glorify the Lord, *
praise him and highly exalt him for ever.

II. The Earth and its Creatures

Let the earth glorify the Lord, *
praise him and highly exalt him for ever.
Glorify the Lord, O mountains and hills,
and all that grows upon the earth, *
praise him and highly exalt him for ever.

Glorify the Lord, O springs of water, seas, and streams, *
O whales and all that move in the waters.
All birds of the air, glorify the Lord, *
praise him and highly exalt him for ever.
Glorify the Lord, O beasts of the wild, *
and all you flocks and herds.
O men and women everywhere, glorify the Lord, *
praise him and highly exalt him for ever.

III. The People of God
Let the people of God glorify the Lord, *
praise him and highly exalt him for ever.
Glorify the Lord, O priests and servants of the Lord, *
praise him and highly exalt him for ever.
Glorify the Lord, O spirits and souls of the righteous, *
praise him and highly exalt him for ever.
You that are holy and humble of heart, glorify the Lord, *
praise him and highly exalt him for ever.[81]

—*The Book of Common Prayer*

Prayers of Confession:

1.

God Our Heavenly Father, You created the world to serve humanity's needs and to lead them to You. By our own fault we have lost the beautiful relationship which we once had with all your creation. Help us to see that by restoring our relationship with You we will also restore it with all Your creation. Give us the grace to see all animals as gifts from You and to treat them with respect, for they are Your creation. We pray for all animals who are suffering as a result of our neglect. May the order You originally established be once again restored to the whole world through the intercession of the Glorious Virgin Mary, the prayers of St. Francis and the merits of Your Son, Our Lord Jesus Christ, Who lives and reigns with You now and forever. Amen.

2.

Lord and heavenly Father
in your hands,
you hold heaven and earth;

all things proceed from your creative will
for you have made each creature
perfect in itself as a sign of your eternal grace;

and yet humankind has corrupted your purpose
turning from light to darkness
and releasing evil in the world.

What you once gave us
has lost its innocence
through our sin
and been marred by our selfishness;

even so you have not despaired of us
but sent your Son
to rescue us and all creation
from the abyss of suffering and death;

yet still we resist your saving work
and frustrate your Spirit within us
and so we pray that this same Spirit
will today renew us and set us right
with ourselves and all creatures.[82]

—Andrew Linzey

3.

Almighty God, without whose knowledge not a sparrow falls to the
ground, we pray to You in Your love to alleviate the sufferings of
Your creatures. Bring to naught the devices of those who treat them

cruelly; and put into the hearts of people a spirit of humanity towards them. Grant to us a truer and deeper understanding of the place of the creatures, not made in the likeness of man, in the scheme of Your creation. Reveal Yourself more fully, as the Lord who saves humankind and animals; and hasten the time when the very creatures will be delivered from vanity and the bondage of corruption and when they will not be hurt or destroyed in all Your holy mountain, through Jesus Christ our compassionate Lord. Amen.[83]

—Source unknown, slightly adapted

4.

Gracious and generous God
 in the beginning you created every living creature;
 birds, cattle, creeping things,
 wild animals and sea monsters,
and you called each one good.
You asked us to care for them,
as you care for us.
We confess that we often fail to care for them,
as you have asked.
We have not treated them as your beloved creations.
Forgive us, Lord,
for putting our own wants and desires
ahead of the needs of animals who have served and loved us;

forgive us for considering them as objects to use

instead as of as beings you made and love.

Teach us to see the faces of our brothers and sisters in domestic animals,

in those who live on the streets and in shelters,

on the farm and in the wild.

May we come to love them as fully as you do.

Amen.

—D.K.F.

Intercessions and Thanksgivings:

1.

Leader: We thank you, God, for the gift of life: for the beauty and wonder of creation, and for our own life which comes from you.

People: Glory to you forever and ever.

Leader: We thank you for the richness of animal life: for fish and birds, insects, reptiles, and mammals.

People: Glory to you forever and ever.

Leader: We thank you for the animals who give us faithful companionship, joy when we are happy, and comfort when we are sad.

People: Glory to you forever and ever.

Leader: We thank you for calling us to care for these animals. May we learn love and respect for all living things.

People: Glory to you forever and ever.[84]

2. *Responsive Blessing of the Animals*

Minister: Surrounded by the animals we love, we remember with gratitude the pets, protectors, and animal companions who have blessed our lives.

People: We give thanks for our childhood pets, who taught us to love and to cry. We give thanks for our children's pets, who help us to teach them responsibility and relationship, and we give thanks for the pets who brighten our days and comfort our nights.

Minister: Surrounded by beloved pets, we remember that many animals suffer.

People: We remember that some animals are hunted or deserted or tortured or hungry. We remember that nature can be cruel and that people can be mean. We remember and want to help.

Minister: Surrounded by the animals we love, we know that many animals contribute to our lives.

People: We give thanks for all those animals who help us: worker animals who guard us and find our lost and guide the blind, the animals who provide us food and clothing, who tote our burdens and entertain us with their antics, and for animals who give their lives to help us learn.

Minister: Spirit of life, help us to remember that we live and work and love among the animals. Help us to be their friends, to love them and care for them and protect them from harm, to thank them when we use their lives for ours. Especially this morning, Spirit of life, bless these animals who are the companions of our lives. Hear our outpouring of love and gratitude for them and help us translate that into love and gratitude for all your creatures.

All: We bless these animals we love. We pledge to care for them tenderly and faithfully, and to remember that we are not alone on the earth. [85]

—Christine Robinson

Blessings:

1.

Fellow creature,

friend and companion;

may God

your creator and preserver,

bless, defend, and keep you

this day and for ever.

Amen.[86]

   —Andrew Linzey

2.

Generous God

whose own self-giving

is reflected in the

love and devotion

of these animal companions;

bless them

with your Spirit,

and make us mindful

of the great responsibility

we bear for

all creatures

dependent upon us

for their welfare;
help us to use
our power over them
for their own benefit
and never selfishly
for our own gain.
Amen.[87]
    —Andrew Linzey

3.
Creator God
your mercies are over
all the earth;
bless this creature, (*Name*),
and help us to delight
in all the works of your hands.
Amen.[88]
    —Andrew Linzey

4.
Holy God
whose loving care
extends to
all living things;

bless and protect
this creature, (*Name*),
which you have put
into our hands
and help us to
cherish *his/her* life
knowing that all life is
precious in your sight.
Amen.[89]

 —Andrew Linzey

5.
Blessed be the Lord
of the earth and the heavens
who loves each living thing
and may the blessing of the Lord
be upon this creature, (*Name*),
by whose providence
all life in earth and heaven
is preserved
and by whose grace
all creation shall be redeemed.
Amen.[90]

 —Andrew Linzey

6.
May this creature
be a blessing to me
and me to *him/her*
in the name of the One
who blesses all those
whose life is a blessing
to others.
Amen.[91]

   —Andrew Linzey

7.
As the leader approaches each pet, the pet's owner speaks the pet's name aloud so that all those gathered may hear. The leader then raises his/her hand above the pet and speaks a word of blessing.

Leader: May God the Creator bless you and keep you through all
         the days of your life!
All: (after each blessing) Thanks be to God!

If some participants have brought mementos of former pets, the leader may touch each memento, while speaking these or similar words.

Leader: May God bless the memory of this pet's presence in your life!

All: Thanks be to God!

If children have brought stuffed animals to receive a blessing, the leader may touch each toy, while speaking these or similar words.

Leader: May this animal's presence be a source of joy and comfort in this child's life!

All: Thanks be to God!

—Linda Witte Henke

Hymns:

All Things Bright and Beautiful
All Creatures of our God and King
Most High, Omnipotent Good Lord
Earth and All Stars
Morning Has Broken

NOTES

1   Andrew Linzey, *Animal Gospel* (Louisville, KY: Westminster John Knox Press, 1998), 12.

2   From *The Complete Works*, edited by A. E. Peers (Wheatampstead, Hertfordshire: Anthony Clarke, 1974) as found in *Animals and Christianity: A Book of Readings*, Andrew Linzey and Tom Regan, editors, (New York: Crossroad, 1990), 93.

3   Albert Schweitzer, *Civilization and Ethics*, by C. T. Campion, editor, (London: Adam & Charles Black, 1967), found in Linzey, *Animals and Christianity*, 119.

4   Dom Ambrose Agius, OSB, M.A., *God's Animals* (The Catholic Study Circle for Animal Welfare 1970), 62.

5   Roberta C. Bondi, *Nick the Cat: Christian Reflections on the Stranger* (Nashville, TN: Abingdon Press, 2001), 10.

6   St. Gregory of Nyssa, "Address on Religious Instruction," found in Andrew Linzey and Tom Regan, *Love the Animals: Meditations and Prayers* (New York: The Crossroad Publishing Company, 1989), 8.

7   St. Gregory Nazianzen, "Hymn to God," from Andrew Linzey and Tom Regan, *Love the Animals*, 14.

8   Nancy Sohn Swartz, illustrated by Melanie Hall, *How Did the Animals Help God?* (Woodstock, VT: Skylight Paths, 2005).

9   St. Bonaventure, *The Soul's Journey into God*, from Andrew Linzey and Tom Regan, *Love the Animals*, 9.

10 Quoted in Andrew Linzey, *Animal Gospel*, pp. 20-21.

11 Alister McGrath, *Incarnation* (Minneapolis: Fortress Press, 2006), 18.

12 From Wesley Granberg-Michaelson, editor, *Tending the Garden: Essays on the Gospel and the Church* (Grand Rapids, MI: William B. Eerdmans, 1987), 87.

13 A.M. Allchin, *God's Presence Makes the World: The Celtic Vision through the Centuries in Wales* (London: Darton, Longman, & Todd, 1997), 12.

14 John Burnaby, "The Belief in Christendom: A Commentary on the Nicene Creed," from Andrew Linzey and Tom Regan, editors, *Animals and Christianity*, 25.

15 Miriam Therese Winter, *eucharist with a small "e"* (Maryknoll, NY: Orbis Books, 2005), 12-13.

16 Roberta Bondi, *Nick the Cat: Christian Reflections on the Stranger*, 137.

17 *Marin Independent Journal*, Tuesday, May 17, 2005.

18 www.pooch.org

19 Desmond Tutu, *God Has a Dream: A Vision of Hope for Our Time* (New York: Doubleday, 2004), 28-9.

20 Ignatius of Loyola, *Spiritual Exercises and Selected Works*, ed. by George E. Ganss, SJ, (New York: Paulist Press, 1991), 163. The following passages from Ignatius come from the same text, 163-5.

21 Jon M. Sweeney, *The St. Francis Prayer Book: A Guide to Deepen Your Spiritual Life* (Brewster, MA: Paraclete Press, 2004), 121.

22 Bruce Malina, "Hospitality," in Paul J. Achtemeier, General editor, *HarperCollins Bible Dictionary* (San Francisco: HarperSanFrancisco, 1985), 440.

23 Edward Hays, *Prayers for the Domestic Church: A Handbook for Worship in the Home* (Easton, KS: Forest of Peace Books, 1979), 24.

24 Paul Sabatier, *The Road to Assisi: The Essential Biography of St. Francis* (Brewster, MA: Paraclete Press, 2003), 166.

25 Timothy Fry, OSB, editor, *The Rule of St. Benedict in English* (Collegeville, MN: The Liturgical Press, 1981), 73.

26   St. Benedict, *The Rule of St. Benedict in English* (Collegeville, MN: The Liturgical Press, 1982), 74.

27   Helen Waddell, *Beasts and Saints* (London: Darton, Longman & Todd, Ltd., 1995), 40.

28   Edward Hays, *Prayers for the Domestic Church*, 34.

29   Anthony F. Chiffolo and Raynes W. Hesse, Jr., *We Thank You, God, for These: Blessings and Prayers for Family Pets* (Mahwah, NJ: Paulist Press, 2003), 37-8.

30   Chiffola and Hesse, *We Thank You, God, for These*, 38.

31   The Monks of New Skete, *I & Dog* (New York: Yorkville Press, 2003), 55.

32   Karla G. Bohmback in David Noel Freedman, editor, *Eerdmans Dictionary of the Bible* (Grand Rapids, MI: William B. Eerdmans Publishing Company, 2000), 945-6.

33   Marc Gellman, *Does God Have a Big Toe?: Stories about Stories in the Bible* (New York: HarperCollins Publishers, 1989), 5.

34   Marc Gellman, *Does God Have a Big Toe?*, 7.

35   "The Naming of Cats," T. S. Eliot, from *Old Possum's Book of Practical Cats*.

36   The Monks of New Skete, *How to be Your Dog's Best Friend*, 195.

37   Andrew Linzey, *Animal Rites: Liturgies of Animal Care* (Cleveland, OH: The Pilgrim Press, 1999), 63-4, slightly adapted.

38   Kathleen Norris, *The Quotidian Mysteries: Landry, Liturgy, and "Women's Work"* (New York: Paulist Press, 1998), 63.

39   The Monks of New Skete, *I & Dog*, 30.

40   Margaret Silf, *The Gift of Prayer: Embracing the Sacred in the Everyday* (New York: BlueBridge, 2004), 12.

41   St. Benedict, *The Rule of St. Benedict in English*, 34.

42   *The Book of Common Prayer* (New York: Oxford University Press, 1979), 258.

43 David N. Bell, *Wholly Animals: A Book of Beastly Tales* (Kalamazoo, MI: Cistercian Publications, 1992), 96.

44 David N. Bell, 31-32.

45 Walter Brueggemann, *Genesis* (Louisville, KY: Westminster John Knox Press, 1982), 32.

46 The Monks of New Skete, *I and Dog*, 6.

47 The Monks of New Skete have an excellent chapter in their book *How to Be Your Dog's Best Friend* (Little Brown). See chapter 13: "The Inner Dimension of Training: In the Beginning is the Relationship," 95–100.

48 David N. Bell, *Wholly Animals*, 62.

49 David N. Bell, *Wholly Animals*, 70-71.

50 The Monks of New Skete, *How to Be Your Dog's Best Friend*, 98.

51 The Monks of New Skete, *How to be Your Dog's Best Friend*, 98-9.

52 Chiffolo and Hesse, *We Thank You, God, for These*, 32-3.

53 Kathleen Norris, *The Quotidian Mysteries*,40.

54 Edward Hays, *Prayers for a Planetary Pilgrim: A Personal Manual for Prayer and Ritual* (Easton, KS: Forest of Peace Books, Inc., 1988), 212.

55 Edward Hays, *Prayers for the Domestic Church*, 65.

56 Michael Counell, editor, 2000 *Years of Prayer* (Harrisburg, PA: Morehouse Publishing, 1999), 73.

57 Anonymous, *The Book of Common Prayer*, 439.

58 *The Book of Common Prayer*, 440.

59 Chiffolo and Hesse, *We Thank You, God, for These*, 40.

60 Anonymous, *The Rule of the Society of Saint John the Evangelist* (Boston: Cowley Publications, 1997), 88.

61 Traditional prayer, from Chiffolo and Hesse, *We Thank You God, for These*, 38.

62 The Theology and Worship Ministry Unit, *Book of Common Worship: Daily Prayer* (Louisville, KY: Westminster/John Knox Press, 1993), 448.

63 The Church of the Province of New Zealand, *A New Zealand Prayer Book* (Auckland, New Zealand: William Collins Publishers Ltd., 1988), 745.

64 Sean Finnegan, *Consecrations, Blessings and Prayers: A Pastoral Companion to the Ritual and to the Book of Blessings* (Norwich, England: Canterbury Press, 2005), 155.

65 Church Missionary Society, 1899, found in Owen Collins, *Classic Christian Prayers* (New York: Random House, 2003), 183.

66 *Enriching Our Worship 2: Ministry with the Sick and Dying, Burial of a Child,* (New York: The Church Pension Fund, 2000), 117.

67 *Enriching Our Worship 2,* 94.

68 Linzey, *Animal Rites,* 106.

69 *New Zealand Prayer Book,* 748.

70 Marcus Borg, *The Heart of Christianity: Rediscovering a Life of Faith* (San Francisco: HarperSanFrancisco, 1993), 182.

71 *Enriching Our Worship 2,* 109.

72 *The Book of Common Prayer,* 501.

73 Edward Hays, *Prayers for the Domestic Church,* 195.

74 Linda Witte Henke, *Marking Time: Christian Rituals For All Our Days* (Harrisburg, PA: Morehouse Publishing, 2001), 142-3.

75 David N. Bell, *Wholly Animals,* 61.

76 Linda Witte Henke, *Marking Time,* 81.

77 Andrew Linzey, *Animal Rites,* 25-7.

78 Abigail Rian Evans, *Healing Liturgies for the Seasons of Life* (Louisville, KY: Westminster John Knox Press, 2004), 80-81. Her source: "Blessing of Home Animals," Excerpted from *Occasional Celebrations of the Anglican Church of Canada* © 1992 by the General Synod of the Anglican Church in Canada, published by the Anglican Book Centre, Toronto.

79   Quoted in Richard Newman, editor, *Bless All Thy Creatures, Lord* (New York: Macmillan Publishing Co., Inc. 1982), 16.

80   Quoted in Richard Newman, editor, *Bless All Thy Creatures, Lord*, 45-6.

81   The Book of Common Prayer, 88-9

82   Andrew Linzey, *Animal Rites*, 45-6.

83   Richard Newman, editor, *Bless All Thy Creatures, Lord*, 47-8.

84   Abigail Rian Evans, *Healing Liturgies for the Seasons of Life*, 81-2.

85   The Rev. Christine Robinson, 1st Unitarian Church of Albuquerque, NM.

86   Andrew Linzey, *Animal Rites*, 102.

87   Andrew Linzey, *Animal Rites*, 102-3.

88   Andrew Linzey, *Animal Rites*, 103.

89   Andrew Linzey, *Animal Rites*, 103.

90   Andrew Linzey, *Animal Rites*, 103.

91   Andrew Linzey, *Animal Rites*, 104.

92   Linda Witte Henke, *Marking Time*, 82.

PERMISSIONS

Excerpts from *Prayers for the Domestic Church* by Edward Hays, © 1979. Used with the permission of the publisher, Forest of Peace, an imprint of Ave Maria Press Inc., Notre Dame, IN 46556. www.forestofpeace.com—cf. notes 23, 28, 55, 73.

Excerpts from *Prayers for a Planetary Pilgrim* by Edward M. Hays, © 1989. Used with permission of the publisher, Forest of Peace, an imprint of Ave Maria Press Inc., Notre Dame, IN 46556. www.forestofpeace.com—cf. notes 54.

Excerpts from *We Thank You, God, for These: Blessings and Prayers for Family Pets*, by Anthony F. Chiffolo and Rayner W. Hesse, Jr., © 2003, Paulist Press. Inc., New York/Mahwah, NJ. Used with permission of Paulist Press. www.paulistpress.com—cf. notes 29, 30, 52, 59.

Reproduced from *Book of Common Worship, Daily Prayer,* 1993. Westminster John Knox Press. Used by permission—cf. note 62.

Copyright material taken from *A New Zealand Prayer Book—He Karakia Mihinare o Aoteearoa.* Used by permission—cf. notes 63, 69.

Excerpts from Andrew Linzey, *Animal Rites: Liturgies of Animal Care,* (Cleveland, OH: The Pilgrim Press, and London: SCM-Canterbury Press, 1999). Used by permission—cf. notes 37, 68, 77, 82, 86, 87, 88, 89, 90, 91.

About Paraclete Press
Who We Are

Paraclete Press is an ecumenical publisher of books and recordings on Christian spirituality. Our publishing represents a full expression of Christian belief and practice—from Catholic to Evangelical, from Protestant to Orthodox.

Paraclete Press is the publishing arm of the Community of Jesus, an ecumenical monastic community in the Benedictine tradition. As such, we are uniquely positioned in the marketplace without connection to a large corporation and with informal relationships to many branches and denominations of faith.

We like it best when people buy our books from booksellers, our partners in successfully reaching as wide an audience as possible.

What We Are Doing
Books

Paraclete Press publishes books that show the richness and depth of what it means to be Christian. Although Benedictine spirituality is at the heart of all that we do, we publish books that reflect the Christian experience across many cultures, time periods, and houses of worship.

We publish books that nourish the vibrant life of the church and its people—books about spiritual practice, formation, history, ideas, and customs.

We have several different series of books within Paraclete Press, including the best-selling *Living Library* series of modernized classic texts; *A Voice from the Monastery*—giving voice to men and women monastics about what it means to live a spiritual life today; award-winning literary faith fiction; and books that explore Judaism and Islam and discover how these faiths inform Christian thought and practice.

Recordings

From Gregorian chant to contemporary American choral works, our music recordings celebrate the richness of sacred choral music through the centuries. Paraclete is proud to distribute the recordings of the internationally acclaimed choir Gloriæ Dei Cantores, who have been praised for their "rapt and fathomless spiritual intensity" by *American Record Guide*, and the Gloriæ Dei Cantores Schola, which specializes in the study and performance of Gregorian chant. Paraclete is also the exclusive North American distributor of the Monastic Choir of St. Peter's Abbey in Solesmes, France, long considered to be a leading authority on Gregorian chant performance.

Learn more about us at our Web site:
www.paracletepress.com, or call us toll-free at
1-800-451-5006.

❖ Also by Debra K. Farrington ❖

Unceasing Prayer
A Beginner's Guide
146 pages, Trade Paper,
ISBN: 1-55725-304-8, $12.95

In the Bible, St. Paul challenges Christians to "pray unceasingly." Is it really possible, in our busy, complicated lives, to pray all the time? In this book, Debra Farrington demonstrates that it is as simple—and as difficult—as recalling God's presence often throughout the day by connecting Scripture with daily activities. Whether you pray regularly or are just beginning, *Unceasing Prayer* will help you to find God everywhere and always.

"A wonderful little book on prayer."
—*The Living Church*

"This book offers a collection of gentle, simple and comforting prayers, gathered from an array of treasured Scripture passages, that will help you find God everywhere and always, touching every sort of human need."
—*Lutheran Woman Today*

Available from most booksellers or through Paraclete Press:
www.paracletepress.com 1-800 451-5006.
Try your local bookstore first.